THE POEMS
of
ST. JOHN
OF THE CROSS

Third Edition

ORIGINAL SPANISH TEXTS

AND

ENGLISH TRANSLATIONS

BY

JOHN FREDERICK NIMS

The University of Chicago Press
Chicago & London

ACKNOWLEDGMENTS

For the Spanish text of these poems I am grateful to the editorial achievements of the late P. Silverio de Santa Teresa: to his *Cántico espiritual y poesías de San Juan de la Cruz, según el códice de Sanlúcar de Barrameda* (1928) and to his monumental *Obras de San Juan de la Cruz* (1929–31). For permission to present the texts here I am grateful to *Editorial "El Monte Carmelo"* (Burgos) and to the help of its gracious *Administrador.*

Earlier versions of some of these poems first appeared in *America, Commonweal, Jubilee, Modern Age, Poetry, Thought,* and *Today.* Earlier versions of "The Spiritual Canticle" and "The Dark Night" appeared in *Sappho to Valéry* (© 1971 by Rutgers University).

The University of Chicago Press, Chicago 60637
The University of Chicago Press, Ltd., London

© 1959, 1968, 1979 by John Frederick Nims
All rights reserved. Third Edition 1979
Phoenix Edition 1979
Printed in the United States of America

83 82 81 80   9 8 7 6 5 4 3 2
ISBN: 0-226-40108-1 (cloth)
0-226-40110-3 (paper)
LCN: 79-12943

CONTENTS

PREFACE TO
THE THIRD EDITION

The poems of San Juan de la Cruz have now been with me for over a quarter of a century. The first of these translations appeared in *Poetry* in 1952. The complete poems were published in 1959 and (revised) in 1968. Here they are again, with the greatest of them again reworked, in a way which I hope brings them closer to the passion and simplicity of the originals.

A poem, says Valéry, is never completed; it is abandoned— given over, after a time, to the flames or to the waste basket. Or to the public. Abandoned in something like despair, as the poet realizes that his words are not living up to what he expected of them. A translation of poetry—except for the occasional miracle—may lead to even more despair, since it is well known that "poetry cannot be translated." The reason is that the poet is not only expressing ideas and feelings, but expressing them in sounds that are a kind of magical equivalent of what they say. The poet is uniting sound and sense. The first thing the translator has to do is wrench the sense from its sound, destroying the magical bond the poet had worked so hard for. When San Juan de la Cruz, for example, is describing a mystical trance of love in which the lover feels that all creation has disappeared and only uncreated beauty remains, he uses two simple words: *cesó todo.* Literally, "all stopped," or "all ceased." But that thought embodied in the languorous blur of *thay-só tóe-though* is not the same as it is when embodied in the abrupt monosyllables of "all stopped." The first is like the soft dissolve of lyrical land-scapes in a movie; the second like the bark of a traffic cop. The very sound becomes part of the meaning; it shows us the manner in which things ceased to be. The poetry of two simple words, so easy to translate literally, is "lost in translation." But more about the translation of poetry—and about the life and work of San Juan—in the "Considerations" printed after the poems.

They have, most of them, been much revised. Some readers feel that revision, which plows and plods, is the enemy of inspiration, which strikes like lightning. Not true: revision is the desire to have a long love affair with inspiration and not just an evening's fling. The Spanish poems, even seen through hours of drudgery and over heaps of worksheets, have never lost their freshness; they seem as miraculous as ever. It is easy to see why so many Spanish poets, poets utterly unlike San Juan de la Cruz, have acclaimed him as the greatest poet of their language. In his far briefer flight, he touches on intensities which I think Dante himself has not ventured near.

At times the extraterrestrial flights of his poetry have reminded me of the imagery of science fiction; at other times of the dreamy sorcery of the surrealists. (No wonder Dali has been attracted to him.) But this year, when Arno Penzias and Robert Wilson have been given a Nobel Prize for their discovery of the lingering warmth of the explosion with which the universe began, another set of images suggests itself. For the poetry of San Juan is about what preceded the Big Bang, about how—to use only an image where we have no fact—a great hand opened in the timeless nowhere to release its rocketry of Time and Space and History, its expanding pyrotechnic display that, eighteen billion years later, is proliferating into new forms with undiminished versatility and brilliance. The great hand opened, San Juan would have said, out of the love and splendor that it wished to

share, and delight and ecstasy were what it had to offer, at least
to anyone courageous enough to survive the Dark Night that is
the dragon of this story. But the human mind is uneasy when it
finds itself outside the pigeonholes of space and time—finds itself
where words like *when* and *outside* and *where* have lost all relevance.

This is the problem that San Juan, as poet, was facing. The
experience he wanted to describe is not a form of physical
reality; not even the subtleties of the subatomic can approach it.
The brain cannot reproduce it by any arrangement of its mole-
cules. There are no words, no mental framework even, for what
he had to say. And yet the poet, as García Lorca reminds
us, is a professor of the five bodily senses. As poet, San Juan had
to put into sensuous terms what was non-sensuous—and to most
of us even non-sense. He had to see the unimaginable love be-
tween his Ineffable Someone and a human being in terms of the
imaginable love between one person and another, between lover
and lover, between bridegroom and bride. His precedent was
the Song of Songs, the most loving and lovable part of the often
dire Old Testament. The Song of Songs has always been suspect
among the decorous because of its imagery, which is frankly
amorous—Saint Teresa tells us that she even knew of religious
who were shocked by it. The poetry of San Juan has been shock-
ing to some for the same reason: how can the love of God for
man, they wonder, be in any way like that of a human lover?
The only bond, San Juan would have said, is in metaphor, which
can suggest much by stating nothing. The Spanish poet and saint
thought his metaphor a proper one, and was so complete a poet,
so accomplished a professor of the five senses, that he never once,
in the great poems, blurred his imagery, mixed his metaphor,
by referring to God as *God* in the pastoral and romantic landscape

he created. God is nearly always *el amado*, the loved one, the one we might affectionately call our "love" or "lover." Or he is *aquel que yo más quiero* ("the one I love the most"), or *mis amores* ("my love"), or *vida mia* ("my life"), or even *carillo* ("darling")—and what puritan could address His Grandeur that way?

But, as the preacher tells us in his worldly-wise pages just before the Song of Songs, "a fool's voice is known by the multitude of words." On to the poems.

I

THE CODEX OF
SANLÚCAR
DE BARRAMEDA

2

CANCIONES ENTRE
el alma y el esposo

Esposa

Adonde te escondiste
amado y me dexaste con gemido?
como el cieruo huiste
auiendome herido
sali tras ti clamando, y eras ydo.

Pastores los que fuerdes
alla por las majadas al otero
si por uentura vierdes
aquel que yo mas quiero
Dezilde que adolesco, peno, y muero.

Buscando mis amores
yre por esos montes y riberas
ni cogere las flores
ni temere las fieras
y passare los fuertes y fronteras.

pregunta a las
criaturas.

O bosques, y espesuras:
Plantadas por la mano del amado
ô prado de verduras
de flores esmaltado
Dezid si por uosotros ha passado.

respuesta de las
criaturas.

Mil gracias deramando
Passo por estos sotos con presura
e yendolos mirando
con sola su figura
Vestidos los dexo de hermosura.

THE SPIRITUAL CANTICLE
Songs between the soul and the bridegroom

Where have you hidden away,
lover, and left me grieving, care on care?
    Hurt me and wouldn't stay
    but off like a deer from there?
I hurried forth imploring the empty air.

The bride

You shepherds, you that rove
over the range where mountains touch the sky,
    if you should meet my love
    —my one love—tell him why
I'm faint, and in a fever, and may die.

I'll wander high and low
after the one I worship; never fear
    the wild things where I go;
    not gather flowers; get clear
of all the mighty and over the frontier.

O fields and woods between,
foliage planted by a lover's hand,
    O bluegrass, evergreen,
    with marigolds japanned,
tell me, has he been lately in your land?

A question to
the creatures

Lavishing left and right
a world of wonders he went streaming by
    the woodland, quick as light.
    And where it touched, his eye
left a new glory on the earth and sky.

Their reply

Esposa.   Ay quien podra sanarme
          acaba de entregarte ya de vero
             no quieras embiarme
             de oy mas ya mensagero
          que no saben dezirme lo que quiero.

             I todos quantos vagan
          de ti me van mil gracias refiriendo
             y todos mas me llagan
             y dexame muriendo
          un no se que que quedan balbuciendo.

             Mas como perseueras
          o vida no viuiendo donde viues
             y haziendo porque mueras
             las flechas que reciues
          de lo que del amado en ti concibes.

             Porque pues has llagado
          aqueste coraçon, no le sanaste?
             y pues me le has robado
             por que assi le dexaste,
          y no tomas el robo que robaste?

             Apaga mis enojos
          pues que ninguno basta a deshazellos
             y veante mis ojos
             pues eres lumbre dellos
          y solo para ti quiero tenellos.

Left me new suffering too!   The bride
Once and for all be really mine, and cure it!
    Yourself! No making do
    with couriers—who'd endure it?
I want your living voice, and these obscure it.

    All that come and go
tell of a thousand wonders, to your credit;
    new rumors—each a blow!
    Like death I dread it.
Something—the telltale tongue, a-stumble, said it.

    How manage breath on breath
so long, my soul, not living where life is?
    Brought low and close to death
    by those arrows of his?
Love was the bow. I know. I've witnesses.

    And wounds to show. You'd cleave
clean to the heart, and never think of healing?
    Steal it, and when you leave
    leave it? What sort of dealing,
to steal and never keep, and yet keep stealing?

    O shorten the long days
of burning thirst—no other love allays them.
    Let my eyes see your face,
    treasure to daze them.
Except for love, it's labor lost to raise them.

O christalina fuente
si en essos tus semblantes plateados
formases de repente
los ojos desseados
que tengo en mis entrañas dibuxados.

Apartalos amado
que voy de buelo:

el esposo.   bueluete paloma
que el cieruo vulnerado
por el otero asoma
al ayre de tu buelo: y fresco toma.

la esposa   Mi amado las montañas
los valles solitarios nemorosos
las insulas estrañas
los rios sonorosos
el siluo de los ayres amorosos.

La noche sosegada
En par de los levantes de la aurora
la musica callada
la soledad sonora
la cena que recrea y enamora.

Nuestro lecho florido
de cueuas de leones enlaçado
en purpura tendido
de paz edificado
de mil escudos de oro coronado.

If only, crystal well,
clear in your silver mirror could arise
   suddenly by some spell
   the long-awaited eyes
sketched in my heart of hearts, but cloudy-wise.

   Love, cover those bright eyes!
I'm lifted! off on air!
            Come settle, dove.   The
                                          bridegroom
   The deer—look yonder—lies
   hurt on the hill above,
drawn by your wing he loves the coolness of.

   My love: the mountains' height,   The bride
forest ravines—their far-away recesses,
   torrents' sonorous weight,
   isles no explorer guesses,
the affectionate air, all whisper and caresses;

   night sunk in a profound
hush, with the stir of dawn about the skies,
   music without a sound,
   a solitude of cries,
a supper of light hearts and lovelit eyes.

   Our bed, a couch of roses,
guarded by lions sunning with their young;
   our room which peace encloses,
   her purple curtains swung;
our wall, with a thousand gold escutcheons hung.

A zaga de tu huella
las jouenes discurren al camino
al toque de centella
al adobado vino
emissiones de balsamo diuino.

En la interior bodega
de mi amado beui; y quando salia
por toda aquesta vega
ya cosa no sabia
y el ganado perdi que antes seguia.

Alli me dio su pecho
alli me enseño sciencia muy sabrosa
y yo le di de hecho
a mi sin dexar cosa:
alli le prometi de ser su esposa.

Mi alma se ha empleado
y todo mi caudal en su seruicio
ya no guardo ganado
ni ya tengo otro officio
que ya solo en amar es mi exercicio.

pues ya si en el exido
de oy mas no fuere vista ni hallada
direis que me he perdido
que andando enamorada
me hize perdidiza, y fui ganada.

Seeing your sandal-mark
girls whirl to the four winds; their faces shine
    stung by a sudden spark,
    flushed with the glorious wine.
Their breath a very heaven—the air's divine!

    Shown deeper than before
in cellars of my love I drank; from there
    went wandering on the moor;
    knew nothing, felt no care;
the sheep I tended once are who knows where?

    There he made gently free;
had honey of revelation to confide.
    There I gave all of me;
    hid nothing, had no pride;
there I promised to become his bride.

    Forever at his door
I gave my heart and soul. My fortune too.
    I've no flock any more,
    no other work in view.
My occupation: love. It's all I do.

    If I'm not seen again
in the old places, on the village ground,
    say of me: lost to men.
    Say I'm adventure-bound
for love's sake. Lost on purpose to be found.

De flores y esmeraldas
en las frescas mañanas escogidas
    haremos las guirnaldas
    en tu amor florecidas
y en un cabello mio entretexidas.

    En solo aquel cabello
que en mi cuello bolar consideraste
    mirastele en mi cuello
    y en el presso quedaste
y en uno de mis ojos te llagaste.

    Quando tu me mirauas
tu gracia en mi tus ojos imprimian
    por esso me adamauas
    y en eso merecian
los mios adorar lo que en ti vian.

    No quieras despreciarme
que si color moreno en mi hallaste
    ya bien puedes mirarme
    despues que me miraste
que gracia y hermosura en mi dexaste.

    Cogednos las raposas
que esta ya florecida nuestra viña,
    entanto que de rosas
    hazemos vna piña
y no paresca nadie en la montiña.

In the cool morning hours
we'll go about for blossoms, sweet to wear;
    match emeralds and weave flowers
    sprung in love's summer air;
I'll give for their entwining the very hair

    curling upon my shoulder.
You loved to see it lifted on the air.
    You loved it, fond beholder
    caught fascinated there;
caught fast by an eye that wounds you unaware.

    Your eyes in mine aglow
printed their living image in my own.
    No wonder, marveling so,
    you loved me, thought me grown
worthier to return the fervor shown.

    But thought me, cheek and brow,
a shade too Moorish, and were slow to praise.
    Only look this way now
    as once before: your gaze
leaves me with lovelier features where it plays.

    Now that the bloom uncloses
catch us the little foxes by the vine,
    as we knit cones of roses
    clever as those of pine.
No trespassing about this hill of mine.

Detente Cierço muerto
ven austro que recuerdas los amores
aspira por mi huerto
y corran sus olores
y pacera el amado entre las flores.

Esposo.

Entrado se ha la esposa
en el ameno huerto desseado
y a su sabor reposa
el cuello reclinado
sobre los dulces braços de el amado.

Debaxo de el mançano
alli comigo fuiste desposada
alli te di la mano
y fuiste reparada
donde tu madre fuera violada.

A las aues ligeras,
leones, cieruos, gamos saltadores,
montes, valles, riberas,
aguas, ayres, ardores,
y miedos de las noches veladores.

Por las amenas liras,
y canto de serenas os conjuro
que cesen vuestras iras,
y no toqueis al muro
porque la esposa duerma mas seguro.

Keep north, you winds of death.
Come, southern wind, for lovers. Come and stir
    the garden with your breath.
    Shake fragrance on the air.
My love will feed among the lilies there.

    She enters, the bride! closes   The
the charming garden that all dreams foretold her;   bridegroom
    in comfort she reposes
    close to my shoulder.
Arms of the lover that she loves enfold her.

    Under the apple tree,
hands joined, we spoke a promise, broke the spell.
    I took you tenderly,
    hurt virgin, made you well
where all the scandal on your mother fell.

    Wings flickering here and there,
lion and gamboling antler, shy gazelle,
    peak, precipice, and shore,
    flame, air, and flooding well,
night-watchman terror, with no good to tell,

    by many a pleasant lyre
and song of sirens I command you, so:
    down with that angry choir!
    All sweet and low
and let the bride sleep deeper. Off you go!

Esposa

O nymphas de Judea
entanto que en las flores, y rosales
el ambar perfumea
morâ en los arabales
y no querais tocar nuestros humbrales.

Escondete Carillo
y mira con tu haz a las montañas
y no quieras dezillo
mas mira las compañas
De la que ua por insulas estrañas.

Esposo.

La blanca palomica
al arca con el ramo se a tornado
y ya la tortolica
al socio desseado
en las riberas verdes a hallado.

En soledad biuia
y en soledad a puesto ya su nido
y en soledad la guia
a solas, su querido
tambien en soledad de amor herido.

Esposa

Gozemonos amado
y vamonos a uer en tu hermosura
al monte u al collado
do mana el agua pura
entremos mas adentro en la espesura.

The bride

Girls of Jerusalem,
now that the breath of roses more and more
    swirls over leaf and stem,
    keep further than before.
Be strangers. And no darkening our door.

Stay hidden close with me,
darling. Look to the mountain; turn your face.
    Finger at lips. But see
    what pretty mates embrace
the passer of fabulous islands in her chase.

The little pearl-white dove
with frond of olive to the Ark returns.
    Wedded, the bird of love
    no longer yearns,
settled above still water, among ferns.

The bridegroom

Hers were the lonely days;
in loneliest of solitudes her nest.
    Her guide on lonesome ways
    her love—ah, loneliest,
that arrow from the desert in his breast.

A celebration, love!
Let's see us in *your* beauty! Jubilees
    on the hill and heights above!
    Cool waters playing! Please,
on with me deep and deeper in the trees!

The bride

y luego a las subidas
cauernas de la piedra, nos iremos
    que estan bien escondidas
    y alli nos entraremos
y el mosto de granadas gustaremos.

Alli me mostrarias
aquello que mi alma pretendia
    y luego me darias
    alli, tu uida mia,
aquello que me diste el otro dia.

El aspirar de el ayre
el canto de la dulce Philomena
    el soto y su donayre
    en la noche serena
con llama que consume y no da pena.

Que nadie lo miraua
Aminadab tan poco parecia
    y el cerco sosegaua
    y la caualleria
a uista de las aguas decendia.

And on to our eyrie then,
in grots of the rock, high, high! Old rumor placed it
    far beyond wit of men.
    Ah but we've traced it,
and wine of the red pomegranate—there we'll taste it!

    There finally you'll show
the very thing my soul was yearning for;
    and the same moment, O
    my dearest life, restore
something you gave the other day: once more

    the breathing of the air,
the nightingale in her affectionate vein,
    woods and the pleasure there
    in night's unruffled reign—
these, and the flames embracing without pain.

    With none around to see.
Aminadab the demon fled offended.
    Above, the cavalry,
    their long siege ended,
sighted the shining waters and descended.

CANCIONES DE

de el alma, que se goza de auer llegado al
alto estado de la perfeccion, que es la
union con Dios por el camino
de la negacion espiritual
De el mesmo
Au-
thor

En una noche obscura
Con ansias en amores inflamada
o dichosa uentura
sali sin ser notada
Estando ya mi casa sosegada

A escuras, y segura
Por la secreta escala disfraçada
o dichosa uentura
a escuras y ençelada
Estando ya mi casa sosegada

En la noche dichosa
En secreto que nadie me ueya.
Ni yo miraua cosa
Sin otra luz y guia
Sino la que en el coraçon ardia

Aquesta me guiaua
Mas cierto que la luz del medio dia
adonde me esperaua
quien yo bien me sabia
En parte donde nadie parecia

THE DARK NIGHT
Songs
of the soul, which rejoices at having reached
that lofty state of perfection :
union with God by the way
of spiritual negation

Once in the dark of night
when love burned bright with yearning, I arose
(O windfall of delight!)
and how I left none knows—
dead to the world my house in deep repose;

in the dark, where all goes right,
thanks to a secret ladder, other clothes,
(O windfall of delight!)
in the dark, enwrapped in those—
dead to the world my house in deep repose.

There in the lucky dark,
none to observe me, darkness far and wide;
no sign for me to mark,
no other light, no guide
except for my heart—the fire, the fire inside!

That led me on
true as the very noon is—truer too!—
to where there waited one
I knew—how well I knew!—
in a place where no one was in view.

O noche que guiaste
o noche amable mas que el aluorada
o noche que juntaste
amado con amada
Amada en el amado transformada

En mi pecho florido
que entero para el solo se guardaua
alli quedó dormido,
y yo le regalaua
y el ventalle de cedros ayre daua

El ayre de la almena
quando yo sus cabellos esparzia
con su mano serena
en mi cuello heria
y todos mis sentidos suspendia.

Quedeme y oluideme
El rostro recline sobre el amado
cesò todo, y dexeme
dexando mi cuidado
Entre las açucenas oluidado.

O dark of night, my guide!
night dearer than anything all your dawns discover!
O night drawing side to side
the loved and lover—
she that the lover loves, lost in the lover!

Upon my flowering breast,
kept for his pleasure garden, his alone,
the lover was sunk in rest;
I cherished him—my own!—
there in air from plumes of the cedar blown.

In air from the castle wall
as my hand in his hair moved lovingly at play,
he let cool fingers fall
—and the fire there where they lay!—
all senses in oblivion drift away.

I stayed, not minding me;
my forehead on the lover I reclined.
Earth ending, I went free,
left all my care behind
among the lilies falling and out of mind.

CANCIONES DEL
Alma en la intima comunicacion
De union de amor De Dios
del mismo auctor.

O llama de amor uiua
que tiernamente hieres
De mi alma en el mas profundo centro
pues ya no eres esquiua
acaba ya si quieres
Rompe la tela deste dulce enquentro.

O cauterio suaue,
o regalada llaga,
O mano blanda, o toque delicado
que a uida eterna sabe
y toda deuda paga,
matando muerte, en vida la as trocado.

O lamparas de fuego
en cuyos resplandores
las profundas cauernas de el sentido
que estaua oscuro, y ciego
con estraños primores
Calor, y luz dan junto a su querido.

Quan manso, y amoroso
recuerdas en mi seno
Donde secretamente solo moras
y en tu aspirar sabroso
de bien y gloria lleno
quan delicadamente me enamoras.

THE LIVING FLAME OF LOVE
Songs
of the soul in its intimate communion
of union with God's love

O living flame of love!
how soothingly you wound
my soul in its profundity—that center
you once made havoc of.
O finish! Take me soon!
Tearing the veil away in love's encounter.

O cautery that freshens!
O treasure of a wound!
Caresses light as air! affectionate palm
with settlement past measure!
the taste of heaven around!
Death done, you lift us living from the tomb.

O lamps of fire, whose light
streams in the cavernous soul:
through mighty hollows, dazzled from above
(once dungeons) see tonight
auroras pole to pole!
lavishing warmth and brilliance on their love!

How lovable, how loving
you waken in my breast,
stirring in nooks, no, none are sharers of!
With your delicious breathing
all health and heavenly rest
how delicately I'm caught afire with love!

COPLAS DEL MISMO
hechas sobre un estasi de harta contempla-
cion

Entreme donde no supe
y quedeme, no sabiendo
toda sciençia traçendiendo.

Yo no supe donde entraua,
pero quando alli me vi,
sin saber donde me estaua
grandes cosas entendi.
no dirè lo que senti
que me quede no sabiendo
toda sciençia traçendiendo.

De paz, y de piedad
era la sciencia perfecta
en profunda soledad
entendida, (via recta)
era cosa tan secreta
que me quede balbuciendo
toda sciencia tracendiendo

Estaua tan embeuido
tan absorto y agenado
que se quedo mi sentido
de todo sentir priuado
y el espiritu dotado
de un entender no entendiendo
toda sciencia tracendiendo.

DEEP RAPTURE
Rimes
after an ecstasy of profound contemplation

I entered—yes but where?
knew nothing being there,
burst the mind's barrier.

I entered—where, who knows?—
but being where I would
(where, who dare suppose?)
great things understood
no telling if I could.
Knew nothing being there,
burst the mind's barrier.

Of goodness and of peace
many a thing I knew;
deserts wide as space
and one road leading through,
clear, yet hidden too.
I stood stammering there—
burst the mind's barrier.

Head swimming with delight,
all-engrossed and fey—
every sound and sight
as dumbfounded lay.
My soul in a strange ray
knew all and nothing there—
burst the mind's barrier.

El que alli llega de uero
de si mismo desfallesce
quanto sabia primero
mucho baxo le paresçe
y su sciencia tanto cresce
que se queda no sabiendo
toda sciencia tracendiendo.

Quanto mas alto se sube
tanto menos se entendia
que es la tenebrosa nube
que a la noche esclarecia
por eso quien la sabia
queda siempre no sabiendo
toda sciençia tracendiendo

Este saber no sabiendo
es de tan alto poder
que los sabios arguyendo
jamas le pueden uencer
que lo llega su saber
a no entender entendiendo
toda sciencia tracendiendo.

Y es de tan alta excellencia
aqueste sumo saber
que no ay facultad, ni sciençia
que le puedan emprender

Once there (the dregs of self
bleeding in shock away)
the clever treat as chaff
their knacks of yesterday;
and thought at wider play
knows nothing being there,
bursts the mind's barrier.

With height on height allowed,
less could I say outright
how blackness of one cloud
was a great moon at night.
Who understands it quite
knows nothing being there,
bursts the mind's barrier.

This knowing that unknows
has mastery so great,
should any sage oppose
he'd blunder in debate,
being no such advocate
as know not knowing there,
burst the mind's barrier.

Of so supreme a kind
this eminence of thought,
as never the mightiest mind
dreamed about or sought.

quien se supiere uencer
con un no saber sabiendo
yra siempre tracendiendo

Y si lo quereis oyr
consiste esta suma sciencia
en un subido sentir
de la diuinal essencia
es obra de su clemencia
hazer quedar no entendiendo
toda sciençia tracendiendo

Souls beyond selfhood caught
know, not knowing, there:
burst the mind's barrier.

If any long for news
of the soul's noblest mode:
What is it but infused
essence of very God?—
whose gentleness allowed
wise unknowing there:
burst the mind's barrier.

COPLAS DEL ALMA
que pena por uer a Dios, de el mis
mo aucthor.

Viuo sin viuir en mi
y de tal manera espero
que muero porque no muero

En mi yo no uiuo ya
y sin Dios biuir no puedo
pues sin el, y sin mi quedo
este biuir que serà?
mil muertes se me harà
pues mi misma vida espero
muriendo porque no muero.

Esta vida que yo viuo
es priuacion de biuir
y assi es contino morir
hasta que biua contigo
oye mi Dios lo que digo
que esta uida no la quiero
que muero porque no muero.

Estando absente de ti,
que vida puedo tener?
sino muerte padescer
la mayor que nunca vi.
lastima tengo de mi
pues de suerte persevero
que muero porque no muero

LIFE NO LIFE
Rimes of the soul
in an agony of longing to see God

Living, and no life in me?
languish in expectancy?—
dying for my dying-day.

Life within me? Not a spark.
Without God's a deadly dark!
Failing him and failing me
how can any life but be
in extremis momently?
Yearning yet for life, I stay
dying for my dying-day.

Seeing that what life I know
is a lack of living, though;
and that dying's all I do
till I come alive in you,
here's a thought to listen to:
life? a thing I'd toss away,
dying for my dying-day.

When I'm far away from you,
how to manage? what to do?
Why encourage breath on breath
and sink deeper in my death?
Pitiful indeed the path
where, though creeping still, I stray—
dying for my dying-day.

El pez que del agua sale
aun de aliuio no caresce
que en la muerte que padesce
al fin la muerte le vale
que muerte aura que se yguale
a mi biuir lastimero
pues si mas viuo mas muero.

Quando me pienso a aliuiar
de uerte en el sacramento
hazeme mas sentimiento
el no te poder gozar
todo es para mas penar
por no verte como quiero
y muero porque no muero

Y si me gozo señor
con esperanca de uerte
en ver que puedo perderte
se me dobla mi dolor
viuiendo en tanto pauor
y esperando como espero
muerome porque no muero

Sacame de aquesta muerte
mi Dios y dame la uida
no me tengas impedida
en este lazo tan fuerte

Fish inveigled from the sea
have relief from misery—
in the dying they endure
death's an everpresent cure.
But what end is torture more
than the penalty I pay,
dying for my dying-day?

When I seem to be content
with you in the sacrament,
suddenly I sink heartsore—
not enjoy where I adore?
Here's one injury the more.
Never see you!—that's to say,
dying for my dying-day.

Dreaming of high heaven, lord,
in hope's vision of reward,
seeing I might never see
doubles my anxiety
till a terror seizes me.
Then I sigh the time away
dying for my dying-day.

From this death deliver me;
give me life in charity!
Must you rope me, head and toe,
in the knots I can't undo,

mira que peno por verte
y mi mal es tan entero
que muero porque no muero

Llorare mi muerte ya
y lamentaré mi vida
en tanto que detenida
por mis peccados està
o mi Dios quando serà
quando yo diga de vero
viuo ya porque no muero

and my heart set all on you?
More and more I feel dismay,
dying for my dying-day.

Sorrow for this death I will,
and lament this living still,
long as I a prisoner in
living make amends for sin.
God, I clamor, tell me when
I can revel?—Death, away!
I'm alive, my dying-day!

OTRAS DEL MISMO A
lo diuino

Tras de un amoroso lançe
y no de esperança falto
bolé tan alto tan alto
que le di a la caça alcançe

Para que yo alcance diese
a aqueste lance diuino
tanto bolar me conuino
que de vista me perdiese
y con todo en este trançe
en el buelo quedé falto
mas el amor fue tan alto
que le di a la caça alcançe

Quando mas alto subia
deslumbrôseme la vista
y la mas fuerte conquista
en escuro se hacia,
mas por ser de amor el lance
di un ciego y oscuro salto
y fui tan alto tan alto
que le di a la caça alcançe

Quanto mas alto llegaua
de este lançe tan subido
tanto mas bajo, y rendido
y abatido me hallaua
Dixe no aura quien alcançe

OF FALCONRY
a lo divino

Upon a quest of love,
hope sturdy and steadfast,
I flew so high, so high,
I caught the prey at last.

In this divine affair,
to triumph—if I might—
I had to soar so high
I vanished out of sight.
Yet in the same ascent
my wings were failing fast—
but love arose so high
I caught the prey at last.

Just when this flight of mine
had reached its highest mark,
my eyes were dazzled so
I conquered in the dark.
I gave a blind black surge
for love—myself surpassed!
and went so high, so high
I caught the prey at last.

The higher up I went
there, in this dizzy game,
the lower I appeared,
more humble, weak, and lame.
I cried, But none can win!

y abatime tanto tanto
que fui tan alto tan alto
que le di a la caça alcançe

Por una estraña manera
mil buelos passe de un buelo
porque esperança de çielo
tanto alcança quanto espera
esperè solo este lançe
y en esperar no fui falto
pues fui tan alto tan alto
que le di a la caça alcançe

and sinking fast oh fast
yet went so high, so high,
I caught the prey at last.

Then—marvelous!—I made
a thousand flights in one,
for hope of heaven will see
all it can wish, be done.
I hoped for this alone;
I hoped; was not downcast.
And went so high, so high,
I caught the prey at last.

OTRAS CANCIONES
A lo diuino (de el mismo autor)
De Christo y el alma.

Un pastorcico solo esta penado
    ageno de plazer y de contento
    y en su pastora puesto el pensamiento
    y el pecho del amor muy lastimado
    No llora por auerle amor llegado
    que no le pena verse asi afligido
    aunque en el coraçon esta herido
    mas llora por pensar que esta oluidado

Que solo de pensar que esta oluidado
    de su bella pastora con gran pena
    se dexa maltratar en tierra agena
    el pecho de el amor muy lastimado
    Y dize el pastorcico, ay desdichado
    de aquel que de mi amor a hecho ausencia
    y no quiere gozar la mi presencia
    y el pecho por su amor muy lastimado.

Y acabo de un gran rato se a encumbrado
    sobre un arbol: do abrio sus braços bellos
    y muerto se a quedado asido dellos
    el pecho de el amor muy lastimado.

MADRIGAL
a lo divino:
of Christ and the soul

Once a young shepherd went off to despond:
how could he dance again? how could he sing?
All of his thoughts to his shepherdess cling,
with love in his heart like a ruinous wound.

The root of his sorrow? No, never the wound:
the lad was a lover and relished the dart
that lodged where it drank the best blood of his heart—
but sighing "Forgotten!" went off to despond.

For only to think it—forgotten by one
beautiful shepherdess!—drove him afar;
cost him a drubbing in foreigners' war,
with love in his heart like a ruinous wound.

The shepherd boy murmured: O curses descend
on the stranger who's stolen my pretty one: she
keeps a cold distance—stares stonily
on the love in my heart like a ruinous wound.

Time passed: on a season he sprang from the ground,
swarmed a tall tree and arms balancing wide
handsomely grappled the tree till he died
of the love in his heart like a ruinous wound.

CANTAR DE LA ALMA
que se huelga de conoscer a Dios
por fee.

Que bien se yo la fonte, que mana, y corre:
    aunque es de noche.

Aquella eterna fonte esta ascondida
    que bien se yo do tiene su manida
    aunque es de noche.

Su origen no lo se, pues no le tiene;
    mas se que todo origen della viene,
    aunque es de noche.

Se que no puede ser cosa tan bella
    y que cielos y tierra beuen della
    aunque es de noche.

Bien se que suelo en ella no se halla
    y que ninguno puede vadealla
    aunque es de noche.

Su claridad nunca es escurecida
    y se que toda luz de ella es uenida
    aunque es de noche.

Se ser tan caudalosos sus corrientes
    que ynfiernos, cielos riegan, y las gentes
    aunque es de noche.

El corriente que nace desta fuente
    bien se que es tan capaz y omnipotente
    aunque es de noche.

SONG OF THE SOUL
whose pleasure is in knowing God
by faith

The spring that brims and ripples oh I know
    in dark of night.

Waters that flow forever and a day
through a lost country—oh I know the way
    in dark of night.

Its origin no knowing, for there's none.
But well I know, from here all sources run
    in dark of night.

No other thing has such delight to give.
Here earth and the wide heavens drink to live
    in dark of night.

Though some would wade, the wave's unforded still.
Nowhere a bottom, measure as you will
    in dark of night.

A stream so clear, and never clouded? Never.
The wellspring of all splendor whatsoever
    in dark of night.

Bounty of waters flooding from this well
invigorates all earth, high heaven, and hell
    in dark of night.

A current the first fountain gave birth to
is also great and what it would, can do
    in dark of night.

El corriente que de estas dos procede
    se que ninguna de ellas le precede
    aunque es de noche.

Aquesta eterna fonte esta escondida
    en este viuo pan por darnos vida
    aunque es de noche.

Aqui se esta llamando a las criaturas
    y de esta agua se hartan aunque a escuras
    porque es de noche.

Aquesta biua fuente que desseo
    en este pan de vida yo la ueo
    aunque de noche.

Two merging currents of the living spring—
from these a third, no less astonishing
 in dark of night.

O fountain surging to submerge again
deep in the living bread that's life to men
 in dark of night.

Song of the waters calling: come and drink.
Come, all you creatures, to the shadowy brink
 in dark of night.

This spring of living water I desire,
here in the bread of life I see entire
 in dark of night.

ROMANCE SOBRE EL
euangelio in principio erat verbum acerca
De la sanctissima trinidad.

En el principio moraua

el uerbo y en Dios biuia

en quien su felicidad

ynfinita posseŷa

el mismo verbo dios era

que el principio se dezia

el moraua en el principio

y principio no tenia

el era el mesmo principio

por eso de el carecia

el verbo se llama hijo

que de el principio nacia

a le siempre concebido

y siempre le concebia

dale siempre su substancia

y siempre se la tenia

y assi la gloria del hijo

es la que en el padre auia

y toda su gloria el padre

en el hijo posseya

como amado en el amante

vno en otro residia

y aquese amor que los une

en lo mismo conuenia

BALLAD I: IN PRINCIPIO
On the most holy trinity

In the beginning the Word
lived in the being of God.
Happy? yes infinitely!
Therein its happiness had.

Seeing it was God, the Word
(as the beginning we call).
In the beginning it lived;
had no beginning at all.

For the beginning it was;
hence what it was, had not.
Son is the word for the Word
of the beginning begot.

The father, time out of mind
begetting, begets him today:
all he possesses, confers;
giving, gives nothing away.

And where does he glory, this son?
In light of the father alone.
And the father delights—? In the son.
So each has come into his own,

as in the lover the loved—
one in the other is so.
This love interfusing the two
may in equality go

con el uno y con el otro

en ygualdad y ualia

Tres personas y un amado

entre todos tres auia

y un amor en todas ellas

y un amante las hazia

y el amante es el amado

en que cada qual viuia

que el ser que los tres posseen

cada qual le poseia

y cada qual de ellos ama

a la que este ser tenia

este ser es cada una

y este solo las unia

en un inefable nudo

que dezir no se sabia

por lo qual era infinito

el amor que las unia

porque un solo amor tres tienen

que su essencia se dezia

que el amor quanto mas uno

tanto mas amor hazia

both with the one as the one—
level in pitch and degree.
Three are the persons, their love
wonderful one-among-three.

Only one love among three!
One love fathering three!
There where the loved is the lover,
life-giving life to the three!

Ponder the range of their power—
each has it all, and alone.
Each is in love with his loving
peers of the luminous zone.

Each is almighty and all,
each and alone is the tie
of the inscrutable union
staggering *wherefore* and *why*.

Infinite love is the link
tying the trio above:
love, sole and yet triple
(such is the mystery thereof);
love, the more single and only,
generates all the more love!

De la comunicacion de las tres personas
2.°

En aquel amor inmenso

que de los dos procedia

palabras de gran regalo

el padre al hijo dezia

de tan profundo deleyte

que nadie las entendia

solo el hijo lo gozaua

que es a quien pertenecia

pero aquello que se entiende

desta manera dezia

nada me contenta hijo

fuera de tu compañia

y si algo me contenta

en ti mismo lo queria

el que a ti mas se parece

a mi mas satisfazia

y el que nada te semeja

en mi nada hallaria

en ti solo me e agradado

o vida de vida mia.

eres lumbre de mi lumbre

eres mi sabiduria

figura de mi substancia

en quien bien me complacia

BALLAD II: OF A COMMUNICATION

In the crescendo of love
that rose from the wonderful two,
the father favored the son
with news of enchanting ado,

inferring a rapture so rich
nobody half understood
but the son, with a jubilant ear
catching what nobody could.

The drift of the father was this
(as near as a mortal can say):
Nothing is sweet to me, son,
whatsoever—if you're away.

Whatever's a cause of delight
is lovable only in you.
Any hint of your look in another's
wins him a welcome too.

Features different from yours
in me little friendliness find.
My pleasure is all your pleasure,
life of the life that is mine!

Light of the light I live by,
knowledge of all I know,
my intimate nature's double—
and my joy in approving you so!

al que a ti te amare hijo
a mi mismo le daria.
y el amor que yo en ti tengo
esse mismo en el pondria
en razon de auer amado
a quien yo tanto queria.

Whoever is your admirer,
son, he has won my heart;
the love that I lavish on you
he shall have, parcel and part:
seeing he loves whom I love
from the depths of my heart.

De la creacion Romance Tercero
Rom. 3.°

Una esposa que te ame
mi hijo darte queria
que por tu ualor meresca
tener nuestra compania
y comer pan a una mesa
de el mesmo que yo comia
por que conosca los bienes
que en tal hijo yo tenia
y se congracie conmigo
de tu gracia y loçania
muncho lo agradesco padre
el hijo le respondia
a la esposa que me dieres
yo mi claridad daria
para que por ella vea
quanto mi padre ualia
y como el ser que posseo
de su ser le recibia
reclinarla e yo en mi braço
y en tu amor se abrasaria
y con eterno deleyte
tu bondad sublimaria.

BALLAD III: OF THE CREATION

My heart dreams of your having,
son, an affectionate bride,
who for the worthiness in you
merits a place at our side:

to break bread at this table,
the same loaf as we two,
and ripen in acquaintance
with traits I always knew,
with handsome ways and graces—
and prize them as I do.

O father, a world of thanks,
the son to the father replied.
The depth of my luminous gaze
I give as a gift to the bride;

I'd have her use it to see
the kind of father you are:
how all that I have to my name
I have from my luckiest star.

To think she will lie in my arms!
Be warmed in the noons of your love!
and in ecstasy never to end
lift radiant carols above!

Prosigue 4.º

Hagase pues dixo el padre
que tu amor lo merecia
y en este dicho que dixo
el mundo criado auia
palacio para la esposa
hecho en gran sabiduria
El qual en dos aposentos
alto, y bajo diuidia
el bajo de diferencias
infinitas componia
mas el alto hermoseaua
de admirable pedreria
por que conosca la esposa
el esposo que tenia
en el alto collocaua
la angelica gerarchia
pero la natura humana
en el baxo la ponia
por ser en su compostura
algo de menor valia
y aunque el ser y los lugares
de esta suerte los partia
pero todos son un cuerpo
de la esposa que dezia

BALLAD IV: OF THE CREATION

Amen, the father smiled;
how love's a cajoler in you.
No sooner said than lo!—
the universe sprang to view.

There was a home for the bride!
a pleasure-house cunningly made!
quarters above and below!
two great levels arrayed!

The lower boldly baroque,
a maze of infinite ways.
The upper thrilling and strange,
diamond dust in a blaze.

To show how noble a groom
(should the bride have a shadow of doubt)
in choirs the father banked
flights of angels about.

Apartments close to the ground
he marked for the race of man—
having fewer claims to worth,
what in the dust began.

Though the palace and all of its gear
the father chose to divide,
they are one: as single a body
as the body itself of the bride.

que el amor de un mesmo esposo

vna esposa los hazia

los de arriba posseian

el esposo en alegria

Los de abajo en esperança

de fee que les infundia

diziendoles que algun tiempo

el los engrandeceria

y que aquella su baxeza

el se la leuantaria

de manera que ninguno

ya la vituperaria

porque en todo semejante

el a ellos se haria

y se uendria con ellos

y con ellos moraria

y que Dios seria hombre

y que el hombre Dios seria

y trataria çon ellos

comeria y beueria

y que con ellos contino

el mismo se quedaria

hasta que se consumase

este siglo que corria

It was one he loved, that lover;
he had eyes for one.
Oh the angels called him truelove
close to their jubilant sun!

Truelove, the earthlings murmured
in hope (with faith for root).
The groom saw, in time future,
radiant changes wrought.

He vowed their meager condition
would be mended: amended so
that none till time had an ending
would find a gibe to throw.

Said he would share their station;
said he would be as they;
mingle in all their dealings;
live there many a day.

God would be man forever;
man would be God-in-man;
weather our hurlyburly,
fed from trencher and can!

Faithful forever, God said;
vowed to be still the same
till the world that trickles away like sand
flare in a waste of flame.

cuando se gozaran juntos

en eterna melodia

Porque el era la cabeça

de la esposa que tenia

a la qual todos los miembros

de los justos juntaria

que son cuerpo de la esposa

a la qual el tomaria

en sus braços tiernamente

y alli su amor la daria

y que assi juntos en uno

al padre la lleuaria

donde de el mesmo deleyte

que Dios goza, gozaria

que como el padre y el hijo

y el que dellos procedia

el uno viue en el otro

assi la esposa seria

que dentro de Dios absorta

vida de Dios viuiria

Something to sing for, that day!
never a dying fall!
He is the bride's best wisdom—
all of her all-in-all.

Limbs by the world far scattered
whole and together awake;
these are his truelove's body;
these will the lover take

into his two arms, soft oh soft,
confiding an idyll of love,
holding her close, to lift her
high to the father above,

there to be rapt as God is,
seized with the same delight—
for even as father and son
and the third, not less in might,

one in the other endure,
so with the fond and fair—
caught into God's great being,
breathing his very air!

Prosigue 5.º R.ce

Con esta buena esperança
que de ariba les uenia
el tedio de sus trauajos
mas leue se les hazia
pero la esperança larga
y el desseo que crecia
de gozarse con su esposo
contino les afligia
por lo qual con oraciones
con sospiros y agonia
con lagrimas y gemidos
le rogauan noche y dia
que ya se determinase
a les dar su compañia
unos dezian o si fuese
en mi tiempo el alegria
otros acaba señor
al que as de embiar, enbia
otros o si ya rompieses
esos cielos y veria
con mis ojos que bajases
y mi llanto cesaria
regad nubes de lo alto
que la tierra lo pedia

BALLAD V:
OF HUNGER FOR THE COMING

Living in lively hope
with that good news from the sky,
earth saw the drudging days
pass more passably by.

But even as hope increased,
as love burned high and higher,
the bride who yearned for the groom
knew anguish of desire.

Praying and praying again,
sighing and pale with pain,
weeping and weeping again,
night and day to exclaim

that he make up his mind and come,
join with her right away.
You could hear: O lucky love,
if I live to see the day!

You could hear: Oh it's long enough!
You know you must come—then come!
You could hear: If a thunderclap
split heaven this minute, and him

I saw with my very eyes!—
no more misery then.
Oh the earth is a dry mouth begging.
Clouds, deliver the rain!

y abrase ya la tierra
que espinas nos producia
y produzga aquella flor
con que ella floreceria
otros dezian o dichoso
el que en tal tiempo seria
que meresca ver a Dios
con los ojos que tenia
y tratarle con sus manos
y andar en su compañia
y gozar de los mysterios
que entonces ordenaria.

Let the stern earth open,
finish with thistle and thorn.
The flower that makes all earth floral—
time for the flower to be born.

You could hear: O lucky lucky
lovers to see that day—
with your own eyes your lover
hastening your way;

stand near enough to touch him,
brush by his very side,
when that mysterious stranger
hints what the night will hide.

Prosigue 6.° R.ce

En aquestos y otros ruegos
gran tiempo pasado auia
pero en los prosteros años
el feruor muncho crecia
quando el viejo simeon
en deseo se encendia
Rogando a Dios que quisiese
dexalle uer este dia
y assi el espiritu santo
al buen viejo respondia
que le daua su palabra
que la muerte no ueria
hasta que la vida uiese
que de arriba decendia
y que el en sus mismas manos
al mismo Dios tomaria
y le tendria en sus braços
y consigo abraçaria.

BALLAD VI: OF SIMEON

Well, in appeals like these
a heavy time went by,
but as the hour drew near
fever-heat ran high;

Simeon, good old man,
love-longing all on fire,
implored that he see the day;
called it his one desire.

Therefore the spirit of God
to the good old man averred
he would never see death at all
(the strange voice gave its word)

till he looked on life itself
and saw the gift from the sky;
swore that the good old man
would dandle the marvelous boy;
that the child embraced in his arms,
in his own two arms would lie.

Prosigue la encar.^{on} R.^e 7.º

Ya que el tiempo era llegado
en que hacerse convenia
el rescate de la esposa
que en duro yugo seruia
debajo de aquella ley
que Moyses dado le auia
El padre con amor tierno
desta manera dezia
ya ues hijo que a tu esposa
a tu ymagen hecho auia
y en lo que a ti se pareçe
contigo bien convenia
pero difiere en la carne
que en tu simple ser no auia
en los amores perfectos
esta ley se requeria
que se haga semejante
el amante a quien queria
que la mayor semejança
mas deleyte contenia
el qual sin duda en tu esposa
grandemente creceria
si te viere semejante
en la carne que tenia

BALLAD VII: OF THE INCARNATION

Now as the season approached
(the date love specified)
for the ransom paid in full,
the shackles struck from the bride

who was forfeit under the law
law-giver Moses made,
the father with melting heart
after this fashion said:

My son, I have found you a bride
of your very sort, you'll find.
You will have good cause to know
you are two of a noble kind,

differing only in flesh
(what are you but a child of sky?).
But the course of true love hints
here is a law will apply:

lovers long to become
as identical as they may;
for the more the two are one,
gayer the gala day.

Delight and love in the bride
speedily would increase
(no question here, my son)
if she saw you a man of flesh.

mi voluntad es la tuya
El hijo le respondia
y la gloria que yo tengo
es tu voluntad ser mia
y a mi me conviene padre
lo que tu alteza dezia
porque por esta manera
tu bondad mas se veria
verase tu gran potencia
justiçia y sabiduria
yrelo a dezir al mundo
y noticia le daria
de tu belleza y dulçura
y de tu soberania
yre a buscar a mi esposa
y sobre mi tomaria
sus fatigas y trauajos
en que tanto padescia
y porque ella vida tenga
yo por ella moriria
y sacandola de el lago
a ti te la bolueria.

I have no will but yours,
the son to the father replied.
My glory is all in this:
I do, and you decide.

It couldn't be other than just
I follow as you provide.
How better let all men see
your charity far and wide?

How better blazon your might,
sweet reason and deep mind?
I'll carry word to the world,
news of a novel kind:
news of beauty and peace,
of sovereignty unconfined.

I go to be close to the bride
and to take on my back (for it's strong)
the weight of the wearisome toil
that bent the poor back for so long.

To make certain-sure of her life
I'll manfully die in her place,
and drawing her safe from the pit
present her alive to your face.

Prosigue 8.º R^ce

Entonces llamó a un archangel
que Sant Gabriel se dezia
y enbiolo a una donzella
que se llamaua maria
de cuyo consentimiento
el mysterio se hazia
en la qual la trinidad
de carne al uerbo vestia
y aunque tres hazen la obra
en el uno se hazia
y quedo el uerbo encarnado
en el vientre de maria
y el que tenia solo padre
ya tambien madre tenia
aunque no como qualquiera
que de varon concebia
que de las entrañas de ella
el su carne recibia
por lo qual hijo de Dios
y de el hombre se dezia

BALLAD VIII: OF THE ANNUNCIATION

It was an angel he beckoned;
it was Gabriel came;
he waved him away on an errand
to Mary—treasure the name.

She must say the right word, this maiden,
for the wonder of wonders to be;
for the Word to be dressed forever
in flesh by the mighty three.

Three had a hand in the work,
but it worked an effect on one.
Who but the Word made flesh?
Where but in Mary's womb?

The son had a father before;
first had a mother then.
Mother yes, but no mother
conceiving as mothers of men.

He had his flesh of her flesh:
so a new life began.
Now the son of the highest
answers to son of man.

Del nacim.^{to} 9.° R^{ce}.

Ya que era llegado el tiempo
en que de nacer auia
assi como desposado
de su thalamo salia
abraçado con su esposa
que en sus braços la traia
al qual la graciosa madre
en un pesebre ponia
entre unos animales
que a la sazon alli auia
los hombres dezian cantares
los angeles melodia
festejando el desposorio
que entre tales dos auia
Pero Dios en el pesebre
alli lloraua y gemia
que heran joyas : que la esposa
al desposorio traya
y la madre estaua en pazmo
el que tal trueque veia
el llanto de el hombre en dios
y en el hombre la alegria
lo qual de el uno y de el otro
tan ageno ser solia.

finis.

BALLAD IX: OF THE NATIVITY

In time it came round, the time
ripe for the birth of a boy.
Much as a bridegroom steps
fresh from the chamber of joy,

arm in arm he arrived
entwining the sweetheart he chose.
Both in a byre at hand
the pleasant mother reposed

among oxen and burros and such
as the winter sky drove in.
How they struck up a tune, those folk!
Sweeter the angels sang!

There was a bridal to chant!
There was a pair well wed!
But why did he sob and sob,
God in his rough-hewn bed?

Such a dazzle of tears!—this gift
all that the bride could bring?
How the mother was struck at so
topsy-turvy a thing:

distress of the flesh, in God!
in man, the pitch of delight!
Pairs never coupled so;
different as day and night.

finis.

Otro de el mismo que va por su
per flumina Babilonis.

Encima de las corrientes

que en babilonia hallaua

alli me sente llorando

alli la tierra regaua

acordandome de ti

o sion a quien amaua

era dulce tu memoria

y con ella mas lloraua

dexe los trages de fiesta

los de trauajo tomaua

y colgue en los verdes sauzes

la musica que lleuaua

poniendola en esperança

de aquello que en ti esperaua

alli me hirio el amor

y el coraçon me sacaua.

Dixele que me matase

pues de tal suerte llagaua

yo me metia en su fuego

sabiendo que me abrasaua

desculpando al auesica

que en el fuego se acabaua

estauame en mi muriendo

y en ti solo respiraua

BALLAD OF BABYLON
Super flumina Babylonis

Brimming of rivers
by Babylon town—
there I sat weeping,
watered the ground.

You in my thoughts, O
Sion my love.
Pleasure of memory
let the tears prove.

Satin I step from,
wear dungaree;
stow the harp high in a
green willow tree.

Stow it in hope there,
looking to you,
who wounded this heart, made
off with it too.

Seeing you've hurt me,
End me! I cry.
Flung me in embers
hoping to die.

Doted to look on
moths in the flame.
Dying myself, I
lived in your name.

en mi por ti me moria
y por ti resusitaua
que la memoria de ti
daua vida i la quitaua
gozauanse los estraños
entre quien catiuo estaua
preguntauanme cantares
de lo que en sion cantaua
canta de Sion un hymno
veamos como sonaua
dezid como en tierra agena
donde por Sion lloraua
cantare yo el alegria
que en Sion se me quedaua
echariala en oluido
si en la agena me gozaua
con mi paladar se junte
la lengua con que hablaua
si de ti yo me oluidare
en la tierra do moraua
Sion por los uerdes ramos
que Babilonia me daua
De mi se oluide mi diestra
que es lo que en ti mas amaua

Dying, died wholly.
Died and awoke.
Lover, your memory
bred me and broke.

Meanwhile the jocular
jailkeepers crow:
Sing us a Siony
ballad of woe!
Chanties of Sionville,
how do they go?

Mourning my country
in faraway air,
sing to a stranger
of Sion so dear?
Harden my heart to her,
high-stepping here?

Tongue, may you fasten
fast to your roof,
when I forget her,
swagger aloof;

by every willow
out Babylon way,
may my harp-fingers
wither away,

si de ti no me acordare

en lo que mas me gozaua

y si yo tuuiere fiesta

y sin ti la festejaua

o hija de Babilonia

misera y desuenturada

bien auenturado era

aquel en quien confiaua

que te a de dar el castigo

que de tu mano lleuaua

y juntara sus pequeños

y a mi porque en ti lloraua

a la piedra que era Christo

por el qual yo te dexaua.

Debetur soli gloria vera

Deo.

when I forget you,
Sion's delight;
when I go revel in
foreigners' night.

Daughter of Babylon,
wretched and doomed,
here's to a hero
conquers your land;
then you'll regret that
lash in your hand.

He'll take his children
and me in my woe
to the rock Jesus—
that's where I go.

To God alone, true
glory.

II

ADDITIONAL POEMS

GLOSA A LO DIVINO

Sin arrimo y con arrimo,
Sin luz y a oscuras viviendo,
Todo me voy consumiendo.

Mi alma está desasida
De toda cosa criada,
Y sobre sí levantada,
Y en una sabrosa vida,
Sólo en su Dios arrimada.
Por eso ya se dirá
La cosa que más estimo,
Que mi alma se ve ya
Sin arrimo y con arrimo.

Y aunque tinieblas padezco
En esta vida mortal,
No es tan crecido mi mal;
Porque, si de luz carezco,
Tengo vida celestial;
Porque el amor de tal vida,
Cuando más ciego va siendo,
Que tiene al alma rendida,
Sin luz y a oscuras viviendo.

Hace tal obra el amor,
Después que le conocí,
Que, si hay bien o mal en mí,

WITHOUT AND WITH MAINSTAY
a lo divino

Without and with mainstay,
no lantern, light of day,
I burn, I burn away.

My spirit in free flight
breaks from the pull of earth,
from ties of human birth,
to breathe a keen delight
suspended from God's worth.
Let the world hear: I hold
my heart's one wish today,
knowing my very soul
without and with mainstay.

Though shadows haunt me still
from man's shape in the sun,
less plaintively they call—
when joys of daylight pall
my heaven is well begun.
Love of that life is such
it thrives in any way:
blind, humble, led by touch,
no lantern, light of day.

Love with its power to charm
so touched my best and worst
that all, even cankered harm,

Todo lo hace de un sabor,
Y al alma transforma en sí;
Y así, en su llama sabrosa,
La cual en mí estoy sintiendo,
Apriesa, sin quedar cosa,
Todo me voy consumiendo.

turned fiber sweet and warm
(being in love immersed).
No wonder resinous fire
leaps sinewy and gay,
as clean to a clean pyre
I burn, I burn away.

GLOSA A LO DIVINO DEL MISMO
AUTOR

Por toda la hermosura
Nunca yo me perderé,
Si no por un no sé qué
Que se alcanza por ventura.

Sabor de bien que es finito,
Lo más que puede llegar,
Es cansar el apetito
Y estragar el paladar;
Y así, por toda dulzura
Nunca yo me perderé,
Sino por un no sé qué
Que se halla por ventura.

El corazón generoso
Nunca cura de parar
Donde se puede pasar,
Sino en más dificultoso;
Nada le causa hartura,
Y sube tanto su fe,
Que gusta de un no sé qué
Que se halla por ventura.

El que de amor adolece,
Del divino ser tocado,
Tiene el gusto tan trocado,
Que a los gustos desfallece;
Como el que con calentura

THE LUCKY DAYS
a lo divino

I'll never pitch away my soul
for any pretty thing,
except for a something—who can tell?—
the lucky days may bring.

Tasty crumbs of being,
tang the tongue can know
are brittles soon decaying,
the palate's overthrow.
I'll never pitch away my soul
for any zesty thing;
only for something—who can tell?—
the lucky days may bring.

What sturdy heart's for lagging
where packs of stragglers go?
contented to be dragging
bottomlands below?
On to attempt the hill,
no time for loitering!
drawn by a something—who can tell?—
the lucky days may bring.

As lovers bright with longing
(for love of Love aglow)
yawn if mere fun comes fawning,
their joy's converted so;
as men in fever smell

Fastidia el manjar que ve,
Y apetece un no sé qué
Que se halla por ventura.

No os maravilléis de aquesto,
Que el gusto se quede tal,
Porque es la causa del mal
Ajena de todo el resto;
Y así, toda criatura
Enajenada se ve,
Y gusta de un no sé qué
Que se halla por ventura.

Que estando la voluntad
De Divinidad tocada,
No puede quedar pagada
Sino con Divinidad;
Mas, por ser tal su hermosura,
Que sólo se ve por fe,
Gústala en un no sé qué
Que se halla por ventura.

Pues de tal enamorado,
Decidme si habréis dolor,
Pues que no tiene sabor
Entre todo lo criado;
Sólo, sin forma y figura,
Sin hallar arrimo y pie,

the best food, shuddering—
these yearn for a something—who can tell?—
the lucky days may bring.

No need to be exclaiming
if these are minded so;
the mark at which they're aiming
is nowhere here below;
no creature-warmth, which all
must soon or late take wing—
their joy in a something—who can tell?—
the lucky days may bring.

The will of a man thrilling
once to God's trumpet tone
can hope for no fulfilling
but in love alone;
in love, that nonpareil
that faith is beckoning—
with joy in a something—who can tell?—
the lucky days may bring.

This lover's of your choosing.
Then say: do humors grow
gloomy at refusing
gusto of things below?
No image shows him well;
no foot, no fin or wing

Gustando allá un no sé qué
Que se halla por ventura.

No penséis que el interior,
Que es de mucha más valía,
Halla gozo y alegría
En lo que acá da sabor;
Mas sobre toda hermosura,
Y lo que es y será y fué,
Gusta de allá un no sé qué
Que se halla por ventura.

Más emplea su cuidado
Quien se quiere aventajar,
En lo que está por ganar,
Que en lo que tiene ganado;
Y así, para más altura
Yo siempre me inclinaré
Sobre todo a un no sé qué
Que se halla por ventura.

Por lo que por el sentido
Puede acá comprehenderse,
Y todo lo que entenderse,
Aunque sea muy subido,
Ni por gracia y hermosura
Yo nunca me perderé,
Sino por un no sé qué
Que se halla por ventura.

can hunt for a something—who can tell?—
the lucky days may bring.

Do any think this yearning
deep in the golden soul
were satisfied, returning
to earth's forsaken shoal?
No season did, none will
show such a lovely thing;
for yonder's something—who can tell?—
the lucky days may bring.

Each greedy bird a-perching
upon earth's dirty store,
gapes at tomorrow urging:
"More! Get more and more!"
But I—an airier tale—
still climb adventuring,
mostly for something—who can tell?—
the lucky days may bring.

Not for all knowledge, throwing
wider the fivefold door,
winds of the spirit blowing
high as a thought can soar,
I'll never pitch away my soul,
nor for a pretty thing—
only for something—who can tell?—
the lucky days may bring.

DEL VERBO DIVINO

Del Verbo divino
La Virgen preñada
Viene de camino
Si le dais posada.

SUMA DE LA PERFECCIÓN

Olvido de lo criado,
Memoria del Criador,
Atención a lo interior
Y estarse amando al Amado.

DIVINE WORD

The wayfaring virgin,
Word in her womb,
comes walking your way—
haven't you room?

THE CAPSULE OF PERFECTION

The whole of creation forgotten;
its Maker remembered forever.
Inward the gaze of the spirit,
forever in love with the Lover.

III

FROM THE CODEX
OF JAÉN

CANCIONES ENTRE EL ALMA Y EL ESPOSO

ESPOSA

¿A dónde te escondiste,
Amado, y me dejaste con gemido?
Como el ciervo huiste,
Habiéndome herido;
Salí tras ti clamando, y eras ido.

Pastores, los que fuerdes
Allá por las majadas al otero,
Si por ventura vierdes
Aquel que yo más quiero,
Decilde que adolezco, peno y muero.

Buscando mis amores,
Iré por esos montes y riberas,
Ni cogeré las flores,
Ni temeré las fieras,
Y pasaré los fuertes y fronteras.

PREGUNTA A LAS CRIATURAS

¡Oh, bosques y espesuras,
Plantadas por la mano del Amado!
¡Oh, prado de verduras,
De flores esmaltado,
Decid si por vosotros ha pasado!

THE SPIRITUAL CANTICLE
Songs between the soul and the bridegroom

THE BRIDE
Where have you hidden away,
lover, and left me grieving, care on care?
Hurt me and wouldn't stay
but off like a deer from there?
I hurried forth imploring the empty air.

You shepherds, you that rove
over the range where mountains touch the sky,
if you should meet my love
—my one love—tell him why
I'm faint, and in a fever, and may die.

I'll wander high and low
after the one I worship; never fear
the wild things where I go;
not gather flowers; get clear
of all the mighty and over the frontier.

A QUESTION TO THE CREATURES
O fields and woods between,
foliage planted by a lover's hand,
O bluegrass, evergreen,
with marigolds japanned,
tell me, has he been lately in your land?

RESPUESTA DE LAS CRIATURAS

Mil gracias derramando,
Pasó por estos sotos con presura,
Y yéndolos mirando,
Con sola su figura
Vestidos los dejó de hermosura.

ESPOSA

¡Ay, quién podrá sanarme!
Acaba de entregarte ya de vero,
No quieras enviarme
De hoy más ya mensajero,
Que no saben decirme lo que quiero.

Y todos cuantos vagan,
De ti me van mil gracias refiriendo,
Y todos más me llagan,
Y déjame muriendo
Un no sé qué que quedan balbuciendo.

Mas, ¿cómo perseveras,
Oh vida, no viviendo donde vives,
Y haciendo porque mueras,
Las flechas que recibes,
De lo que del Amado en ti concibes?

¿Por qué, pues has llagado
Aqueste corazón, no le sanaste?
Y pues me le has robado,
¿Por qué así le dejaste,
Y no tomas el robo que robaste?

THEIR REPLY

Lavishing left and right
a world of wonders he went streaming by
the woodland, quick as light.
And where it touched, his eye
left a new glory on the earth and sky.

THE BRIDE

Left me new suffering too!
Once and for all be really mine, and cure it!
Yourself! No making do
with couriers— who'd endure it?
I want your living voice, and these obscure it.

All that come and go
tell of a thousand wonders, to your credit;
new rumors—each a blow!
Like death I dread it.
Something—the telltale tongue, a-stumble, said it.

How manage breath on breath
so long, my soul, not living where life is?
Brought low and close to death
by those arrows of his?
Love was the bow. I know. I've witnesses.

And wounds to show. You'd cleave
clean to the heart, and never think of healing?
Steal it, and when you leave
leave it? What sort of dealing,
to steal and never keep, and yet keep stealing?

Apaga mis enojos,
Pues que ninguno basta a deshacellos,
Y véante mis ojos,
Pues eres lumbre de ellos,
Y sólo para ti quiero tenellos.

Descubre tu presencia,
Y máteme tu vista y hermosura;
Mira que la dolencia
De amor, que no se cura
Sino con la presencia y la figura.

¡Oh, cristalina fuente,
Si en esos tus semblantes plateados,
Formases de repente
Los ojos deseados,
Que tengo en mis entrañas dibujados!

Apártalos, Amado,
Que voy de vuelo.

ESPOSO

Vuélvete, paloma,
Que el ciervo vulnerado
Por el otero asoma,
Al aire de tu vuelo, y fresco toma.

ESPOSA

Mi Amado, las montañas,
Los valles solitarios nemorosos,
Las ínsulas extrañas,
Los ríos sonorosos,
El silbo de los aires amorosos,

O shorten the long days
of burning thirst—no other love allays them.
Let my eyes see your face,
treasure to daze them.
Except for love, it's labor lost to raise them.

Appear here at my side,
though I die dazzled in a blaze of grace.
Look at love's invalid,
heartsick, a failing case—
only one chance of comfort: face to face.

If only, crystal well,
clear in your silver mirror could arise
suddenly by some spell
the long-awaited eyes
sketched in my heart of hearts, but cloudy-wise.

Love, cover those bright eyes!
I'm lifted! off on air!

THE BRIDEGROOM

Come settle, dove.
The deer—look yonder—lies
hurt on the hill above,
drawn by your wing he loves the coolness of.

THE BRIDE

My love: the mountains' height,
forest ravines—their far-away recesses,
torrents' sonorous weight,
isles no explorer guesses,
the affectionate air, all whisper and caresses;

La noche sosegada
En par de los levantes del aurora,
La música callada,
La soledad sonora,
La cena que recrea y enamora.

Cazadnos las raposas,
Que está ya florecida nuestra viña,
En tanto que de rosas
Hacemos una piña,
Y no parezca nadie en la montiña.

Detente, Cierzo muerto;
Ven, Austro, que recuerdas los amores,
Aspira por mi huerto,
Y corran tus olores,
Y pacerá el Amado entre las flores.

¡Oh, ninfas de Judea,
En tanto que en las flores y rosales
El ámbar perfumea,
Morá en los arrabales,
Y no queráis tocar nuestros umbrales!

Escóndete, Carillo,
Y mira con tu haz a las montañas,
Y no quieras decillo;
Mas mira las compañas
De la que va por ínsulas extrañas.

night sunk in a profound
hush, with the stir of dawn about the skies,
music without a sound,
a solitude of cries,
a supper of light hearts and lovelit eyes.

Now that the bloom uncloses
catch us the little foxes by the vine,
as we knit cones of roses
clever as those of pine.
No trespassing about this hill of mine.

Keep north, you winds of death.
Come, southern wind, for lovers. Come and stir
the garden with your breath.
Shake fragrance on the air.
My love will feed among the lilies there.

Girls of Jerusalem,
now that the breath of roses more and more
swirls over leaf and stem,
keep further than before.
Be strangers. And no darkening our door.

Stay hidden close with me,
darling. Look to the mountain; turn your face.
Finger at lips. But see
what pretty mates embrace
the passer of fabulous islands in her chase.

ESPOSO

A las aves ligeras,
Leones, ciervos, gamos saltadores,
Montes, valles, riberas,
Aguas, aires, ardores
Y miedos de las noches veladores:

Por las amenas liras,
Y canto de serenas os conjuro,
Que cesen vuestras iras,
Y no toquéis al muro,
Porque la Esposa duerma más seguro.

Entrádose ha la Esposa
En el ameno huerto deseado,
Y a su sabor reposa,
El cuello reclinado
Sobre los dulces brazos del Amado.

Debajo del manzano,
Allí conmigo fuiste desposada,
Allí te dí la mano,
Y fuiste reparada
Donde tu madre fuera violada.

ESPOSA

Nuestro lecho florido
De cuevas de leones enlazado,
En púrpura tendido,
De paz edificado,
De mil escudos de oro coronado.

THE BRIDEGROOM

Wings flickering here and there,
lion and gamboling antler, shy gazelle,
peak, precipice, and shore,
flame, air, and flooding well,
night-watchman terror, with no good to tell,

by many a pleasant lyre
and song of sirens I command you, so:
down with that angry choir!
All sweet and low
and let the bride sleep deeper. Off you go!

She enters, the bride! closes
the charming garden that all dreams foretold her;
in comfort she reposes
close to my shoulder.
Arms of the lover that she loves enfold her.

Under the apple tree,
hands joined, we spoke a promise, broke the spell.
I took you tenderly,
hurt virgin, made you well
where all the scandal on your mother fell.

THE BRIDE

Our bed, a couch of roses,
guarded by lions sunning with their young;
our room which peace encloses,
her purple curtains swung;
our wall, with a thousand gold escutcheons hung.

A zaga de tu huella
Las jóvenes discurren al camino
Al toque de centella,
Al adobado vino,
Emisiones de bálsamo divino.

En la interior bodega
De mi amado bebí, y cuando salía
Por toda aquesta vega,
Ya cosa no sabía
Y el ganado perdí que antes seguía.

Allí me dió su pecho,
Allí me enseñó ciencia muy sabrosa,
Y yo le dí de hecho
A mí, sin dejar cosa,
Allí le prometí de ser su esposa.

Mi alma se ha empleado,
Y todo mi caudal en su servicio;
Ya no guardo ganado,
Ni ya tengo otro oficio,
Que ya sólo en amar es mi ejercicio.

Pues ya si en el ejido
De hoy más no fuere vista ni hallada,
Diréis que me he perdido;
Que andando enamorada,
Me hice perdidiza, y fuí ganada.

Seeing your sandal-mark
girls whirl to the four winds; their faces shine
stung by a sudden spark,
flushed with the glorious wine.
Their breath a very heaven—the air's divine!

Shown deeper than before
in cellars of my love I drank; from there
went wandering on the moor;
knew nothing, felt no care;
the sheep I tended once are who knows where?

There he made gently free;
had honey of revelation to confide.
There I gave all of me;
hid nothing, had no pride;
there I promised to become his bride.

Forever at his door
I gave my heart and soul. My fortune too.
I've no flock any more,
no other work in view.
My occupation: love. It's all I do.

If I'm not seen again
in the old places, on the village ground,
say of me: lost to men.
Say I'm adventure-bound
for love's sake. Lost on purpose to be found.

De flores y esmeraldas,
En las frescas mañanas escogidas,
Haremos las guirnaldas,
En tu amor florecidas,
Y en un cabello mío entretejidas.

En solo aquel cabello
Que en mi cuello volar consideraste,
Mirástele en mi cuello,
Y en él preso quedaste,
Y en uno de mis ojos te llagaste.

Cuando tú me mirabas,
Su gracia en mí tus ojos imprimían:
Por eso me adamabas,
Y en eso merecían
Los míos adorar lo que en ti vían!

No quieras despreciarme,
Que si color moreno en mí hallaste,
Ya bien puedes mirarme,
Después que me miraste,
Que gracia y hermosura en mí dejaste.

ESPOSO

La blanca palomica
Al arca con el ramo se ha tornado,
Y ya la tortolica
Al socio deseado
En las riberas verdes ha hallado.

In the cool morning hours
we'll go about for blossoms, sweet to wear;
match emeralds and weave flowers
sprung in love's summer air;
I'll give for their entwining the very hair

curling upon my shoulder.
You loved to see it lifted on the air.
You loved it, fond beholder
caught fascinated there;
caught fast by an eye that wounds you unaware.

Your eyes in mine aglow
printed their living image in my own.
No wonder, marveling so,
you loved me, thought me grown
worthier to return the fervor shown.

But thought me, cheek and brow,
a shade too Moorish, and were slow to praise.
Only look this way now
as once before: your gaze
leaves me with lovelier features where it plays.

THE BRIDEGROOM

The little pearl-white dove
with frond of olive to the Ark returns.
Wedded, the bird of love
no longer yearns,
settled above still water, among ferns.

En soledad vivía,
Y en soledad ha puesto ya su nido,
Y en soledad la guía
A solas su querido,
También en soledad de amor herido.

ESPOSA

Gocémonos, Amado,
Y vámonos a ver en tu hermosura
Al monte y al collado,
Do mana el agua pura;
Entremos más adentro en la espesura.

Y luego a las subidas
Cavernas de la piedra nos iremos,
Que están bien escondidas,
Y allí nos entraremos,
Y el mosto de granadas gustaremos.

Allí me mostrarías
Aquello que mi alma pretendía,
Y luego me darías
Allí tú, vida mía,
Aquello que me diste el otro día.

El aspirar del aire,
El canto de la dulce Filomena,
El soto y su donaire,
En la noche serena
Con llama que consume y no da pena.

Hers were the lonely days;
in loneliest of solitudes her nest.
Her guide on lonesome ways
her love—ah, loneliest,
that arrow from the desert in his breast.

THE BRIDE

A celebration, love!
Let's see us in *your* beauty! Jubilees
on the hill and heights above!
Cool waters playing! Please,
on with me deep and deeper in the trees!

And on to our eyrie then,
in grots of the rock, high, high! Old rumor placed it
far beyond wit of men.
Ah but we've traced it,
and wine of the red pomegranate—there we'll taste it!

There finally you'll show
the very thing my soul was yearning for;
and the same moment, O
my dearest life, restore
something you gave the other day: once more

the breathing of the air,
the nightingale in her affectionate vein,
woods and the pleasure there
in night's unruffled reign—
these, and the flames embracing without pain.

Que nadie lo miraba,
Aminadab tampoco parecía,
Y el cerco sosegaba,
Y la caballería
A vista de las aguas descendía.

With none around to see.
Aminadab the demon fled offended.
Above, the cavalry,
their long siege ended,
sighted the shining waters and descended.

IV

NOTES

CONSIDERATIONS

I

The best account in English of the life of St. John of the Cross had been Gerald Brenan's *Horizon* article—the first of two—in May, 1947. Twenty-five years later, in the light of recent scholarship, Mr. Brenan brought his account up to date in his *St. John of the Cross: His Life and Poetry*, published with the translations of Lynda Nicholson (Cambridge University Press, 1973). The remarks that follow are indebted to Mr. Brenan's work.

Born in 1542 in a village of Old Castile, Juan de Yepes was brought up in great poverty by a widowed mother. As a youth he worked as carpenter, tailor, painter; he had some training in art and later drew a remarkable crucifixion which Salvador Dali has made famous. He loved music, particularly the popular songs of the people. In school he probably became acquainted with the Latin poets; he would have heard all around him the Spanish *romances* or folk ballads, unrivaled in Europe.

Becoming at twenty-one a Carmelite friar, he spent four years at the University of Salamanca. Biblical studies obviously claimed a good part of his time, since "no protestant divine ever quoted Scripture more often." Just before leaving the university he met Teresa of Ávila, then past fifty, and became interested in her project for the reform of the Carmelite order: its return to a more primitive rule that would stress prayer and contemplation. In 1568, as Juan de la Cruz, he took his vows with the Reformed Carmelites. For about the next ten years his existence, in a simple country monastery and as confessor to the convent at Ávila, was outwardly uneventful.

Then in 1577 he became the key figure in a cloak-and-dagger episode. Because of the violent hostility of the unreformed Carmelites and a more far-reaching suspicion of Reformed Carmelite practices

(St. John himself had been denounced to the Inquisition) he was kidnaped and dragged off to the Priory at Toledo—the large building, now destroyed, to the right of the bridge in El Greco's Plan of Toledo. There he was shut in a gloomy, ill-smelling little closet; half starved; permitted no change of his flea-ridden clothing for eight months, and beaten by his unreformed brethren at frequent intervals with such zeal that his shoulders were crippled for life.

In the midst of his sufferings, he heard one evening from the street below a popular song about unhappy love—sixteenth-century blues:

> Muérome de amores,
> Carillo, qué haré?
> —Que te mueras, alahé!

Always susceptible to the charm of music and poetry, capable of hearing them *a lo divino* (as symbolizing the love between God and man), St. John, enraptured by the sadness and beauty of that worldly song, was himself inspired to expression. His greatest lyrics, the *Cántico* and the *Noche*, and some others were written in whole or in part during these months in prison, precisely *nel mezzo del cammin di nostra vita*.

His escape, the following August, was as melodramatic as the kidnaping eight months earlier. With ropes twisted from strips of blanket and tunic, he let himself down from a dizzy height into the darkness. Somehow, after a stunning fall and mysterious assistance over a wall too high to climb, he found his way, through the blackness of a strange city, to the Reformed Carmelite Convent; there he was taken in "looking like an image of death," and given pears stewed with cinnamon. That he regarded his poetry as more than a pastime is shown, the very day of his escape, by his dictating some verses he had composed in prison but had been unable to write down.

The following spring was spent at a mountain hermitage, rugged and beautiful, in Andalusia. Here he completed the lyrics, and his dazzling career as poet, which had opened not many months before, was "practically finished." Then followed three years at Baeza, farther down the Guadalquivír. The charm of landscape, all the forces of nature, were an unfailing inspiration to him—what saves this oldest of clichés is that in him they actually inspired something: praise of God for the beauty of created being and for the knowledge of Him which we derive from it; this he referred to, with great affection, as *the knowledge of the evening,* distinct from the daylight knowledge of God in Himself.

In 1582 he went to Granada as prior for three quiet years; on the hillside not far from the Alhambra, "with one of the most beautiful views in the world before him," he wrote his long commentaries on the poems. In the years that followed, as Vicar General for Andalusia, he traveled widely, by burro, through southern Spain, going even as far as Lisbon and Madrid, sleeping, like Don Quijote, in the open air or by the brawling, overcrowded inns. In 1588, as new dangers threatened in the order, he became prior at Segovia, a post he held until May of 1591, when his insistence on chapter elections by secret ballot led to his disgrace and removal to a solitary spot in Andalusia. To destroy him once and for all, enemies within his own order set about collecting or fabricating evidence. Feeling ran so high that, rather than risk guilt by association, people with letters or papers from him thought it safer to destroy them. Only his final illness saved him from further persecution: in September of 1591 he was brought low with fever and terrible ulcers; these proving uncontrollable, on December 14th of that year he died, his voice rising from the rotted flesh in delight at the beauties of the Song of Songs. Almost immediately there were wild public demonstrations in his favor. Popularly recognized as a saint even in his own lifetime, he was canonized in 1726, proclaimed a Doctor of the Church in 1926. There are no specific references to the external events of his life in his poetry, which is surely rich, however, in such reminiscences as Brenan points out in speaking of the last lines of the *Cántico*:

> *Y el cerco sosegaba,*
> *Y la caballería*
> *A vista de las aguas descendía.*

I do not think that in the whole of Spanish poetry there is a passage that calls up so vividly the Castilian-Andalusian scene: the line of horses or mules descending slowly to the river; the vague suggestion of frontier warfare, now over: that sense of endless repetition, of something that has been done countless times before being done again, which is the gift of Spain to the restless and progressive nations. In those last two wonderful lines with their gently reassuring fall, the horses descending within sight of the waters are lifted out of time and made the symbol of the peace of this Heracleitan land of eternal recurrence.

Nowhere in St. John's work or in what we know of his life does he indicate the slightest sense of embarrassment or self-consciousness (or pride) about his poetry, or the slightest regret when he came to write no more. Apparently he had no scruples about its being in conflict with other interests: he urged the religious under him to improvise verses *a lo divino* in their times of recreation. He left it with no grand gestures of renunciation. At times he enjoyed indulging his facility: some of his verses are mere exuberant improvisings. When moved by delight and love to express himself by way of poetry, he did so as no other ever has; when moved by delight and love to pass beyond that stage, he went gaily into *la música callada*. One feels from his writings that no man has ever found a richer wonderland of delight or wasteland of darkness than St. John found in his own soul, often at altitudes quite beyond poetry. Probably during much of his life the intensity of his experience was too great to need or admit of expression. What Yeats has written about the poet and human love here comes to mind : had the poet been successful in love

> who can say
> What would have shaken from the sieve?
> I might have thrown poor words away
> And been content to live.

As indeed St. John was, though "content" is too weak a word, and though his life was not the life his companions—and still less the strangers around him—were able to see.

"There are certain kinds of sanctity," said St. Teresa in one of her marvelously barbed remarks, "I do not understand." These twisted sorts of sanctity would include that of people who turn to religion and "God" out of weak blood or nightmare terrors or *mal protesi nervi* or plain hatred of the world : the feeling that if they had had the making of it, many loose ends in existence would have been tucked in with more niceness and propriety. St. John's holiness was far from being of this sort. He saw everything created as fresh and beautiful ; saw, without Hopkins' torment, "the dearest freshness deep down things." The fields, the flowers, the animals, men and angels, wine, companionship, poetry, the singing voice—all were beautiful. Most rapturous of all was human love. He saw the evening world as very good, but saw beyond it something realer and more thrilling. We fall in love, we others, with our bright particular star, he with the infinite galaxies of Night.

II

Dámaso Alonso tells us that it is the unanimous opinion of the Spaniards who know about such matters that St. John of the Cross is the greatest Spanish poet.[1] Pedro Salinas says that his best works, with their "incomparable sensual power," are "charged with poetic potency like no other work written in this world."[2] Jorge Guillén thinks that his three best poems—the first three in this edition—"form a series which is perhaps the highest culmination of Spanish poetry."[3] García Lorca too is passionate in his praise. In his essay on *duende*,[4] Lorca tells us that there are artists sponsored by an Angel that guides, endows, dazzles, shedding his grace in mid-air. There are those sponsored by the Muse, who comes "bearing landscapes of columns and the false taste of laurel." There is also a third type, which has *duende*: the Andalusian term for that mysterious power "that all may feel and no philosophy may explain," that all Dionysian artists at their best have, the bullfighter "who hurls his heart against the horns" or the flamenco singer "like a woman possessed, her face blasted like a medieval weeper . . . feeling the power rise from the very soles of her feet." *Duende* is

> the mystery, the roots that probe through the mire we all know of, and do not understand, but which furnishes us with whatever is sustaining in art. . . . In all Arabic music, in the dances, songs, elegies of Arabia, the coming of the *Duende* is greeted by fervent outcries of *Allah! Allah! . . .* so close to the *Olé! Olé!* of our bull rings that who is to say they are not actually the same; and in all the songs of southern Spain the appearance of the *Duende* is followed by heartfelt exclamations of *God alive!*— profound, human, tender, the cry of communion with God through the medium of the five senses . . .

St. John of the Cross belongs not with the Angel, as we might suspect, nor with the Muse: taking him with two of the greatest names in

---

[1] *La Poesía de San Juan de la Cruz* (3rd ed.; Madrid: Ediciones de Aguilar, S.A., 1958).
[2] *Reality and the Poet in Spanish Poetry* (Baltimore: Johns Hopkins Press, 1966).
[3] *Language and Poetry* (Cambridge: Harvard University Press, 1961).
[4] "The Duende: Theory and Divertissement" in *Poet in New York*, trans. Ben Belitt (New York: Grove Press, Inc., 1955), pp. 154–66.

Spanish poetry Lorca acclaims him thus: "The Muse of Góngora and the Angel of Garcilaso must yield up the laurel wreath when the *Duende* of St. John of the Cross passes by . . ."

And is it just accidental, the remarkable similarity between the tone and imagery of St. John's greatest poems and Lorca's brilliant account of the poet at work?[5]

> The poet who embarks on the creation of the poem (as I know by experience), begins with the aimless sensation of a hunter about to embark on a night hunt through the remotest of forests. Unaccountable dread stirs in his heart. . . . Then the poet is off on the chase. Delicate breezes chill the lenses of his eyes. The moon, curved like a horn of soft metal, calls in the silence of the topmost branches. White stags appear in the clearing between the tree trunks. Absolute night withdraws in a curtain of whispers. Water flickers in the reeds, quiet and deep . . .

My present concern is with St. John as poet, not as mystic. Mysticism itself cannot write poetry; it can only stammer about the ineffable. Probably no abnormal state, no kind of "inspiration," can give us a work of art. We have to be awake to describe a dream, says Valéry—who reminds us also that one does not have to be going sixty miles an hour at the time he is designing a locomotive. García Lorca believes that no great artist has ever worked in a state of fever.

Hundreds of anecdotes about the masters show that they were canny craftsmen more often than mysterious winged creatures. St. John of the Cross, certainly, was a technician as well as a visionary. When asked by a nun if his poems were the result of inspiration or of his own hard work, he answered, as any good poet would: of both. "Daughter, some of them God gave me and some I looked for myself."

The poet, García Lorca reminds us, is a professor of the five senses. It may be amazing to some that whereas St. John's mystical quest drove

---

[5] "The Poetic Image in Don Luis de Góngora" in *Poet in New York*, p. 175.

him into a dark night where the senses had to be abandoned, in the world of his poetry he never left them. "We are immediately fascinated," says Guillén, "by these forms that do not break with the laws of our world." To describe the love and love-longing between God and man, St. John, in his greatest poem, never uses the word *God* at all, but looks for a metaphor that will not break with the laws of our world. He finds it in what he considers the best thing we can know : human love—as in the Song of Songs, certainly his favorite poetry and his favorite part of the Bible. The narrative and imagery of the *Cántico* are based on the pursuit of courtship, the promise of betrothal, the fruition of marriage. Even in his own time the theme must have drawn raised eyebrows and embarrassed giggles. St. Teresa tells of a sermon on the same theme broken by ignorant chortles from the congregation. She tells too of nuns who were scandalized by the Song of Songs :

> You may think that in these Canticles there are some things which could have been said otherwise. Our dullness being what it is, I should not be surprised if you did : I have heard some people say that they actually tried not to listen to them. O God, how miserable is our condition ! We are like poisonous things that make poison of all they eat . . . !

But the puritan penumbra had not fallen on St. John of the Cross—it seems never to have occurred to him that the language of human passion might be an improper metaphor for divine love. Nor is he fevered by it; critics have never ceased to wonder at the freshness, sweetness, and delicacy with which he has handled the theme.

Always metaphor-conscious, he explains that he is using this or that as a figure of speech, or that he is using such and such a figure so as not to mix the metaphor. He does not blur levels of reality; in his great poems there are no obtrusive signposts pointing skyward. Once we look at the poetry with a workman's eye, perhaps what we notice first is what Guillén calls coherence of metaphor. But St. John is careful too about lesser things. Once he writes out for us a technical description of a stanza form, complete with number of syllables and rhyme scheme. In his best work he keeps to a tight pattern, generally with lines of seven and eleven syllables.

"The sound," said Robert Frost, "is the gold in the ore." St. John, who loved music and folk song, was sensitive also to the analogous music of speech, and to the way sound can dramatize meaning as well as state it. In his famous showpiece line—not the kind of trick any poet would want to do often—he tells us that the things of this world afford only a kind of vague and stammering communion with God. The line, in natural Spanish, stammers too :

> *Un no sé qué que quedan balbuciendo.*

That he was taken by the expressiveness of the repeated *k*'s is shown by what is apparently a first attempt at the effect :

> *que me quedé balbuciendo.*

Dámaso Alonso, in a study that does not discount the mysticism, provides some discerning analyses of expressive sound effects, and Emilio Orozco has written several pages on sounds in the last stanzas of "The Spiritual Canticle" that "humanize" and "materialize" speech by the very sensation of physical adherence in the lip movements that produce them.[6]

All of this suggests that when St. John was writing his poems his attention was not on his "thought" alone. The relation between thought and sound has been described by Paul Valéry, the one who has perhaps gone deepest into the poetic process :[7]

---

[6] *Poesía y Mística, Introducción a la Lírica de San Juan de la Cruz* (Madrid : Guadarrama, 1959).

[7] *The Art of Poetry*, trans. D. Folliot (New York : Random House Vintage Book, 1961), p. 291–92.

If he is a true poet, he will nearly always sacrifice to form (which, after all, is the end and act itself, with its organic necessities) any thought that cannot be dissolved into the poem because it requires him to use words or phrases foreign to the poetic tone. An intimate alliance of sound and sense, which is the essential characteristic of poetic expression, can be obtained only at the expense of something—that is, thought. Conversely, all thought which has to define and justify itself to the extreme limit dissociates and frees itself from rhythm, numbers, and resonance—in a word, from all pursuit of the sensuous qualities of speech. A proof does not sing. . . .

In his poems St. John was not proving; he was singing. His mystical experiences, he insists, cannot logically be described at all, "for it would be ignorance to think that sayings of love understood mystically, such as those of the present stanzas, can be fairly explained by words of any kind"—and this because the human mind is not programed to process data of a nature beyond its own. St. John explains why he preferred poetry :[8]

Who can express that which He makes them desire? None certainly; not even the very souls through which He passes. It is for this reason that by means of figures, comparisons and similitudes, they let something of that which they feel overflow and utter secret mysteries from the abundance of the Spirit, rather than rationally explain these things. These similitudes, unless they are read with the simplicity of the spirit of love and understanding they embody, seem to be nonsense rather than reasonable expression, as may be seen in the divine Songs of Solomon and other books of the Divine Scripture, in which the Holy Spirit, since he cannot express the fullness of his meaning in common language, utters mysteries in strange figures and similitudes . . .

But since he had been asked—as what poet is not?—what his lines meant, he did undertake to elucidate the three great poems—with

---

[8] Translated from the *Prólogo* to the *Cántico Espiritual* in *Obras de San Juan de la Cruz,* ed. P. Silverio de Santa Teresa, O.C.D. (Burgos: El Monte Carmelo, 1930), Vol. III, pp. 3–4.

the caution, however, that his readers remember that poetry can say better than prose what there is to be said. What resulted is probably the most detailed self-explication ever written. There are about one hundred pages on his twenty-four-line "The Living Flame of Love," and then a revised explication about fifteen pages longer. Both the "Ascent of Mount Carmel" and "The Dark Night," nearly five hundred pages in all, start out as explications of a short lyric on the dark night—and never get beyond line 10 of the poem.

One example should make clear what his method is. In stanzas 29 and 30 of "The Spiritual Canticle" we have:

> Wings flickering here and there,
> lion and gamboling antler, shy gazelle,
> peak, precipice, and shore,
> flame, air, and flooding well,
> night-watchman terror, with no good to tell,
>
> by many a pleasant lyre
> and song of sirens I command you, so: . . .

The prose exposition is as follows:[9]

1. The Spouse continues, and in these two stanzas describes how, by means of the pleasant lyres, which stand for the sweetness habitually enjoyed in this condition, and also by the sirens' song, which stands for the delight that He always has in the soul, He has just brought to conclusion all the operations and passions of the soul which before were a certain impediment to quiet pleasure and sweetness. These things, He now says, are the digressions of the imagination, and He commands them to cease. Furthermore, he brings under control the two natural faculties, which somewhat afflicted the soul before, and which are wrath and concupiscence. And also, by means of these lyres and this song, He shows how in this condition, as far as possible in this life, the three faculties

---

[9] *Ibid.,* pp. 138–40.

of the soul—understanding, will, and memory—are brought to perfection and put in working order. It is also described here how the four passions of the soul—grief, hope, joy, and fear—are tempered and controlled by means of the satisfaction which the soul possesses, signified by the pleasant lyres and the sirens' song, as we shall now explain. All these impediments God now wishes to cease, so that the soul, at her own will and without interruption, may have full enjoyment of the delight, peace, and sweetness of this union.

Wings flickering here and there,

2. He calls the digressions of the imagination "wings flickering" since they are light and swift in their flight first to one place and then another. When the will is quietly enjoying delightful communications from the Beloved, they are likely to annoy it and by their swift flights to disturb its joy. These the Beloved says that he commands by the "pleasant lyre." This means that since the sweetness and delight of the soul are now so rich and frequent and strong that they could not hinder it as they used to do, when it had not reached so high a condition, they are to cease their restless flights, their impetuous dartings and extravagances. This is to be taken in the same way as other parts of the stanza which we have to explicate, such as:

lion and gamboling antler, shy gazelle,

3. By the "lion" is understood the acrimonies and impetuosities of the irascible faculty, which is as bold and brave in its acts as lions are. By the "antler" and "gazelle" is meant the other faculty of the soul, which is the concupiscible, the power of desiring, which has two effects: one of cowardice and one of boldness. It produces the effects of cowardice when it finds that things are unpleasant, for then it withdraws into itself and is timid, and in this it is like a gazelle, for even as these animals possess the concupiscible faculty to a greater degree than other animals, so too they are very timid and shy. It produces the effect of boldness when it finds that things are pleasant, for then it no longer retreats nor is timid,

but boldly advances to lust after and accept them with its passions. In regard to boldness this faculty is compared to the "gamboling antler" of animals which have such concupiscence toward that which they desire that they not only run toward it but leap after it, for which reason they are called "gamboling."

4. So that, in commanding the lion, the Spouse restrains impetuous and extravagant wrath, and in commanding the gazelle He strengthens the concupiscible faculty with respect to the cowardice and timidity of spirit which caused it to shrink before; and in commanding the gamboling antler, He satisfies and quiets the desires and appetites which roamed restlessly about before, gamboling like antlered beasts from one thing to another, in order to satisfy the concupiscence which is now satisfied by the pleasant lyre, whose sweetness it enjoys, and by the song of sirens, upon whose delight it feeds. It is to be noted that it is not wrath and concupiscence which the Spouse commands here, for these faculties are never absent from the soul, but their troublesome and tumultuous acts, which are denoted by the lion, the shy gazelle, and the gamboling antler; it is necessary that in this condition they should cease.

> peak, precipice, and shore,

By these three words are denoted the vicious and disorderly acts of the three faculties of the soul—memory, understanding, and will—which are vicious and disorderly when they are carried to a high extreme, and also when they are at a low or deficient extreme, or even when they are not at either extreme, but tend toward one or the other; and so the peaks, which are very high, stand for acts which are extreme in being over-violent. By the precipices, which go down low . . .

A comparison between the stanzas and their explication illustrates as well as anything I know the difference between poetry and prose.[10] In the poem, meanings are suggested by imagery and music; in the

---

[10] *Cf.* Sister Rose Maria Icaza, *The Stylistic Relationship Between Poetry and Prose in the Cántico Espiritual of San Juan de la Cruz.* (Washington, D.C.: Catholic University of America Press, 1957.)

prose, they are rather drearily spelled out and overelaborated. St. John does not mix the two modes: the lion of the poem is a lion, as real as Rilke's: *Zähne zeigt und Zunge*. It is not "the lion of acrimony," or anything so hybrid, for the poet, like Ezra Pound much later, believed that the natural object is always the adequate symbol. His poems are, as Guillén observed, "almost completely uncontaminated by allegory."

"But if you meant 'the acrimonies and impetuosities of the irascible faculty'," a literal reader might have objected, "why talk about a lion? Aren't you being unfaithful to your own thought?" The poet might have replied that he was not trying to express a thought; he was looking for an image. The prose makes it clear that there were many things he might have said for everything he did say in the poems: from the great welter of the nonverbalizable he selected an image that condensed as much as possible and did not make nonsense of the image next to it. What he selected was influenced too by a cadence, or by his need for a certain number of syllables or, every few words, by his need for a rhyme.

III

All of these remarks are relevant to the problem of translating poetry: there are still readers who insist on the "thought," which seems more important to them than it ever did to the poet. Even experts may forget: one critic objected to earlier versions of these translations because the translator had not remembered, he said, that every word of St. John was to be "taken literally." Yet time and again in his prose St. John insists that nothing is to be taken literally; he does not even take himself literally, and on one occasion declares that although he is explaining his poem in a certain way, "there is no reason why anyone should be limited to this explanation."

Although the prose is inferior to the poetry in expressiveness—in imagery, drama, music, passion—it has claims of its own, as throwing light on the poetry. Yet there have been translators of the poetry who have not consulted it. Critics too have shown a general unawareness: one reproved these translations for making the rivers too noisy and the islands too remote and strange, in stanza 13 of the "Canticle." The poet was merely thinking, the critic assured us, of the little Tajo with its clumps of mud and willows. He was not: the prose tells us that these rivers "assail and submerge all they meet . . . their sound is such as to drown out and take the place of all other sounds . . ." and it tells us that "the strange islands are surrounded by the ocean and are far away over the sea . . ." It is true that obligations of rhyme and rhythm and the difference in length between corresponding expressions in Spanish and English have sometimes led me to add this or that, but generally what I have added (to the great poems) is something the poet tells us he had in mind—and might just as well have said in place of what he did say had the demands of his rhyme and rhythm persuaded it.

All I have said above implies a theory of the translation of poetry: the translator has an obligation to form as well as to content, and if rhythm meant as much to the poet as "thought" did, or if he felt a sound effect worth achieving, the translator should at least be aware of that effect and work toward it, if he can. He will frequently fail; it is a commonplace that poetry cannot be translated. But perhaps it can sometimes be re-created, as Rilke re-created Valéry, or as Valéry re-created Virgil. Without being Rilke or Valéry, one can try to work as they did, and not merely be content to give the thought of a poet who was not primarily concerned with thought. How many drab little translations one sees commended for their "fidelity"—a fidelity, alas, as unimpressive as that of a wife too ugly to make free with.

In Mallarmé's famous summary, poetry is not made out of ideas, but out of words. Perhaps the same may be said for its translation. It is surprising how many translators have not known, or not tried to find out, what kind of words St. John used. Experts who do know—such as Dámaso Alonso—tell us that the poet liked simple everyday expressions, popular, colloquial words that occur in folk song and that the country people would be likely to use. Rarely a literary word. But in the translations one comes across diction like "Whither hast vanishèd, Belovèd?" or "Oh who my grief can mend?" or "O hapless-happy plight!" Is this even good English, let alone colloquial English?

Much is to be said for a theory of the translation of poetry that might be described as that of equivalent effect—like what Valéry had in mind in his essay on a French translation of St. John of the Cross: "This is really to *translate*, which is to reconstitute as nearly as possible the *effect* of a certain *cause*—here, a text in Spanish—by means of *another cause*, a text in French."[11]

The first version of this translation of "The Spiritual Canticle" appeared in *Poetry* in 1952. It was considerably revised for *The Poems of St. John of the Cross* (1959). In 1968 this poem and nearly all of the others were further revised, and in some cases entirely rewritten. The three great poems were then reworked the most, as they deserve: about three-fourths of the translated text was rewritten. Nearly half of the lines in the four poems most would consider next in importance were also changed. "Of Falconry" was entirely redone in a manner probably closer to the author's; and about nine-tenths of the less important "The Lucky Days" was new. Only about thirty changes were made in the nine theological ballads. In 1971, "The Spiritual Canticle" and "The Dark Night" were again reworked for inclusion in my *Sappho to Valéry: Poems in Translation* (Rutgers University Press). And now, in 1979, these two and "The Living Flame of Love" have undergone extensive revision—sometimes with the restoration of lines from earlier editions but more often with the substitution of new phrasing. All of this work was done in the hope of getting closer to the real feeling of the Spanish poetry—as far as it could be realized in a language whose qualities are quite different from those of the Spanish.

---

11 *Op. cit.*, p. 286.

THE SPANISH TEXT

Although such distinguished editions as those of P. Gerardo (1912–1914) and P. Silverio (1929–1931) have gone far toward arriving at an authoritative text of St. John of the Cross, Dámaso Alonso was still able, in 1958, to make a strong plea for the *"verdadera—e indispensable—edición científica."* The edition of the Biblioteca de Autores Cristianos (Madrid, 1950) does not claim final validity: it admits that with the possibility of new codices turning up "one cannot yet declare any text definitive."

For present purposes, it seems desirable to offer a Spanish text as close as possible to what the poet actually wrote, one that will show as little as possible the well-intentioned but sometimes meddling editorial hand—the more so as no text so virgin has yet been presented along with an English translation.

These assumptions pointed clearly to the text at present *más autorizado* according to Dámaso Alonso and *de indiscutible autoridad* for the B.A.C. editors: the text of the Codex of Sanlúcar de Barrameda, preserved in the Carmelite convent of the town of that name near Cadiz. It contains the *Cántico espiritual* and the principal poems, apparently transcribed by a careful and devoted hand. What gives the manuscript its supreme value is the fact that St. John himself (authorities almost without exception agree) examined it *"con cariño"*—read it through, corrected errors, made notes and additions in his own hand—in short, proofread it—many years before the poems were published. All this not only guarantees the authenticity of the text but provides an irresistible emotional appeal: we are seeing the very text the poet saw and approved.

If there is any disadvantage in using sixteenth-century Spanish instead of the modernizations we are familiar with, the fascination of the codex more than countervails the initial difficulty, which in any case is slight. This, after all, is the way we are used to seeing—and indeed insist on seeing—such writers as Jonson, Donne, and Webster, roughly St. John's contemporaries, in sound modern editions.

In Part I, then, I follow the Codex of Sanlúcar for the poems it contains. The text of the four poems of Part II and the Jaén redaction of the *Cántico* (Part III) follow the standard edition of P. Silverio de Santa Teresa.

THE CODEX OF SANLÚCAR DE BARRAMEDA:

PRESENT EDITION

The Codex of Sanlúcar de Barrameda was published in an *edición fototipográfica* (as *Cántico espiritual y poesías de San Juan de la Cruz*) edited by P. Silverio de Santa Teresa, C.D., Tipografía El Monte Carmelo, Burgos, 1928. The two-volume edition reproduces the codex on the left-hand pages, prints the text on the right. It contains the *Cántico espiritual* (poem and prose explication), and, following this, "*las principales poesías que conocemos del Santo.*" The transcription in the Spanish edition exactly follows the manuscript, we are told; if there have been any slips they can easily be corrected by looking across the page (*Si algún desliz se ha escapado, es fácil de subsanar por la reproducción fotográfica*). As a matter of fact the transcribers have not been over-careful: there are at least forty errors, mostly trivial, in the text of the poems alone. When there has been a discrepancy between the photographed manuscript and the transcription, I have followed the manuscript.

Mine does not aspire to be a scholarly edition of the codex; it aims merely at transferring the text of the poems soundly and clearly to the printed page. I have first of all corrected the errors of the printed transcription, some of which are apparently misprints (*estale y* for *esta ley,* etc.) and most of which are unimportant misreadings or modernizings of the manuscript. Besides these misreadings, the transcriber sometimes takes for an acute accent the slash or hook which is written, apparently at random, over many *i*'s, especially in the termination of the imperfect tense. I find no basis for this in the manuscript; these slashes are used indifferently over *i*'s that would or would not have the written accent today.

I have put each new poem on a new page, rather than follow the pagination of the manuscript, which begins a new poem directly at the close of the preceding one. Changing the pagination, I have omitted the catchwords occasionally used. In the ballads, a capital letter is used eight times at the beginning of a line only because it is the first line on its page: these now otiose capitals have been removed. The symbol $\bar{q}$, used half a dozen times, in lengthened to *que*; the appropriate nasal is added to three or four *ū*'s. Five or six times a period or other mark clearly mistaken or misleading is removed—a period, for example, in what can only be the middle of a sentence. About a dozen flamboyant capitals (all *A*'s or *D*'s) in midsentence have been humbled. In the twelfth stanza of the *Cántico*, where there is a change of speaker, I have transferred to the margin the speech-prefix, which had been written in, above midline, as a correction, and divided the stanza between the speakers. In the twenty-eighth stanza I have corrected the erroneous *su* to *tu*, which is correctly given twice when the line is quoted in the prose explication. (In the codex the poem is written out in full; then each stanza is quoted separately for explication; under the stanza-explications individual lines are quoted. When the text differs, I follow the text of the poem given in full, with the exception just mentioned.) I have bestowed a cedilla on the *c* of *disfraçada* in the *Noche oscura*, and corrected the irregular indentations of the third stanza of that poem. Otherwise the text printed here gives exactly what the author himself let stand.

ORTHOGRAPHY

The sixteenth-century orthography of the Sanlúcar codex is not more remote than that of English texts of the period. Though words are not necessarily spelled the same even when repeated in the same line, spelling is far more regular than English spelling contemporary with it. There were almost no written accents; punctuation was much lighter than today. The Sanlúcar pages are pleasantly clean and uncluttered when compared with those of modern editions, fairly bristling with all kinds of pointers nudging and nagging at the text.

Y and *i*, *u* and *v* may change about, just as in these lines attributed to Raleigh:

> To serue, to liue, to looke vpon those eies,
> To looke, to liue, to kisse that heauenlie hand . . .

So we find *ymagen*, *yguale*, *deleyte*, *posseẏa*, *oyr*, *yre* (*iré*), *yrelo*, etc.; on the other hand *y* ("and") is sometimes written *i*. We find *vivo* or *uiuo*, *ver* or *uer*, *va* or *ua*, *aves* or *aues*. The *u-v* interchange is complicated by the fact that in the Spanish *v* and *b* stand for the same sound ("*ningún puro castellano sabe hazer diferencia*," it was observed in 1558). Modern *enviar* may appear as *embiar* or *enbiar*; *vivir* as *biuir*, *volvería* as *bolueria*, *vuelo* as *buelo*, *volar* as *bolar*, etc. *B* may also appear as *u*: the imperfect ending is commonly written *-aua* instead of *-aba*, though in one long series of imperfects the Sanlúcar text uses both forms. We find *auer* for *haber*, *aura* for *habrá*, *auia* for *había*, *auiendome* for *habiéndome*, *beui* for *bebi*, *caualleria* for *caballería*, *siluo* for *silbo*, *trauajo* for *trabajo*, etc.

J and *x* had the same sound and were used interchangeably: *baxo*, *debaxo*, *exercicio*, *exido*, *dixe*, *dexar*, *dexo* (*dejó*), *dexame* (*déjame*), *dexeme* (*dejéme*), etc.

Z is found where today we are used to *c*, as in *hazer* (*haziendo*, *hize*, etc.), and *dezir* (*dize*, *dezia*, *dezilde*, etc.). *Z* (or *c*) may appear as *ç*: *braço*, *mançano*, *coraçon*, *esperança*, *caça*, *lançe*, etc.

The familiar *h* is missing in *oy*, *e*, *a*, etc. But *eran* is found as *heran*.

G is found for *j* in *ageno*, *trages*, *mensagero*, etc.

Qu is found for *cu* in *quan* (*cuán*), *quando*, *quanto*, *qual*, *enquentro*, etc.

Some letters are doubled: *assi* (*así*), *desseo*, *esso*, *fee*, *passe* (*pasé*), *passo* (*pasó*), *posseo*, etc. Or the reverse: *arabales*, *ariba*, *deramando*, etc.

Some words now combined were left separate: *entrado se* (*entrádose*), *a le* (*hale*), *de el*, etc. Or the reverse: *ençelada*, *acabo*, *della*, *dellos*, *desta*, etc.

A few old or familiar forms are used: *comigo* (*conmigo*), *contino* (*continuo*), *mesmo* (*mismo*), *muncho* (*mucho*), *Sant* (*San*). A few other forms no longer current will be readily recognized: *Christo*, *gerarchia* (*jerarquía*), *nymphas*, *prosteros* (*postreros*), *thalamo* (*tálamo*).

NOTES ON THE POEMS

The following notes are frequently indebted to:

PSJ   Dámaso Alonso, *La Poesía de San Juan de la Cruz*. Madrid, 1946; third edition, 1958.

PE   *Poesía española, ensayo de métodos y límites estilísticos*. Madrid, 1950.

Gerald Brenan,   *St. John of the Cross: His Life and Poetry*. Cambridge, 1973.

LSP   *The Literature of the Spanish People*. Cambridge, 1953.

The Spiritual Canticle (pp. 2–17)

Much of the poem was written during St. John's painful imprisonment at Toledo in 1578: the influence of that harsh environment has been felt in the powerful reverberations of the opening lines. In prison the poet wrote as far as the stanza beginning "*O ninfas de Judea*"—the reference is probably to the stanzaic order of the first version. Of the remaining stanzas, all but the last five were written, not long after his escape, at Baeza—"one likes to think . . . by the banks of the Guadalimar, in the woods of the Granja de Santa Ana" (P. Silverio-Peers). The last five stanzas were written at Granada (where he resided from 1582 to 1585) under the influence of an access of delight and love he felt to hear a nun report that her prayers were given to "considering the beauty of God and . . . rejoicing that he has such beauty."

St. John of the Cross, though he felt that poetry gave fuller expression to (or richer intimations of) his experiences than prose exposition could hope to (the latter can give only "the least part of that which they contain") was prevailed on to write a prose explication of the poem, stanza-by-stanza, line-by-line. Probably while examining the poem—itself all élan and ardor—with the critic's eye, he decided that a rearrangement of many of the stanzas would bring them in closer correspondence with the mystical progress he was describing. The result is the "second redaction" or "new Spiritual Canticle" of the Codex of Jaén (cf. pp. 98–115 and the notes to those pages). Although the second version may be more satisfactory to the student of mystical theology, the first has long been recognized as the finer poem. For a study in English of the two versions, cf. I. I. Macdonald, "The Two Versions of the *Cántico Espiritual*," Mod. Lang. Notes, XXV, pp. 165–184 (April, 1930).

Echoes of St. John's favorite poetry, that of the *Song of Songs*, are of course everywhere in the "Canticle," which is indebted also to Garcilaso (and through him to Italian Renaissance poetry) for some features of the pastoral treatment, for the hendecasyllabic rhythm of the long lines, and for the stanza known as the *lira* (used also in "The Dark Night")—a form devised by Bernardo Tasso to suggest Horatian effects in a stressed language. The *lira* was used also by Fray Luis de Leon, who lectured at Salamanca during the years St. John of the Cross was there. The peculiar feature of this combination of seven- and eleven-syllable lines consists in "the way in which the last long line of each stanza, coming as it does after two short ones, the second of which rhymes with it, rolls forward like the fringe of a wave to reach a new high-water mark." (Brenan, LSP, pp. 157–8.)

The general impression of the "Spiritual Canticle" has been eloquently described by Gerald Brenan in the second of his *Horizon* articles:

> The *Cántico* starts with a cry of longing and anguish, but almost at once this changes to an air-borne feeling of lightness, clarity, exhilaration, speed of movement. There is a sense of travel and adventure: mountains, rivers, valleys, dawns, breezes, "strange islands" come and go: lions, antelopes, birds, flowers are seen and left behind. There are gusts of passion and tenderness and then the clear Castilian air grows

heavy for a moment with the scent of cedar wood and lilies, whilst the lovers, in walled gardens or rocky caves or on castle battlements, meet together to perform their mysterious rites. Yet the voluptuousness which blows in from the East is tempered to an astonishing delicacy. This poetry is virginal; and there is at times a penetrating strangeness of tone that recalls—as very little poetry really recalls—the pathos of dreams."

The Dark Night (pp. 18–21)

Said, though without positive evidence, to have been written in prison; written, at any rate, not long after. For Jean Baruzi (*Saint Jean de la Croix et le problème de l'expérience mystique*) the night-symbolism of this poem (and the following one) constitutes St. John's most original and profound intuition. The influence of Arabic mysticism here and elsewhere has been suggested but not established. To expound the poem ("each stanza . . . and the lines of each stanza") St. John wrote "The Ascent of Mount Carmel" and "The Dark Night of the Soul." Both are incomplete; nearly 500 pages of explication cover little more than the first ten lines of the poem. For a recent study, cf. Leo Spitzer, "Three Poems on Ecstasy (John Donne, St. John of the Cross, Richard Wagner)" in *A Method of Interpreting Literature*.

The Living Flame of Love (pp. 22–23)

This poem belongs to the Granada period, probably to 1583 or 1584. The poet has himself explained the stanzaic structure in a famous note near the beginning of the prose explication of this poem: "The structure of these *liras* are [sic] like those which in Boscán are given a divine meaning [he quotes three lines] and in which there are six lines, the fourth riming with the first, the fifth with the second, and the sixth with the third." Alonso (PE, pp. 287–9) analyzes this curious note, with its uncorrected syntax, its reference to the joint *Obras de Boscán y Garcilaso* simply as "*Boscán*" and the reference to *liras*— actually the stanza form he uses is the first half of a complicated *canción* stanza of Garcilaso. The lines quoted are not from the original, but from the pious revision of Sebastián de Córdoba, who rewrote

Garcilaso *a lo divino*. Alonso (PSJ, p. 146) thinks the lamps of the third stanza—which he considers one of the poet's most concentrated and significant images—were suggested by a phrase of the *Song of Songs*: "lampades ejus, lampades ignis atque flammarum."

In the last line of stanza 2, most editors have preferred the comma after *matando* rather than after *muerte*.

Deep Rapture (pp. 24–29)

A *villancico* of the familiar Castilian type. Typically a popular dance-song, the *villancico* develops an initial theme of from two to four lines (the *estribillo*) in stanzas that end with a line or two of the theme. Alonso suspects that the theme (often borrowed or traditional) was in this case invented by the poet. Basic in the thought of St. John (and one does not have to read far in the poet to agree with Alonso in this) is this juxtaposition of opposites, this recourse to contraries in the struggle against the limitations of human speech. In the decade between PSJ and PE Alonso's admiration for this poem increased from "a masterpiece in a minor key" to "nothing less than one of the best definitions of our national *irracionalidad*, and one of the peaks of the whole range of Spanish poetry." The phrase *"no entender entendiendo"* is from the work of St. Teresa.

Life No Life (pp. 30–35)

This poem, like the preceding one, develops, with refrain, an initial theme—glossed also by St. Teresa. Versions attributed to her contain some stanzas apparently interpolated from the text of St. John. The paradoxical life-death theme, which flourished in courtly tradition back at least to the troubadours, is of course a universal commonplace, from Euripides' queries about life-as-death and death-as-life (in fragments from the lost *Polyidus* and *Phrixus*) to T. S. Eliot's "death by water" and "hour of our birth."

Of Falconry (pp. 36–39)

A long line of Spanish poems had seen the course of human love and its pursuit in falconry images; some of these *a lo divino*. This poem of St. John was suggested by a rather poor anonymous verse evidently about human love: St. John has taken for his theme the first four lines of the older poem with the change of only a word or two and developed them independently. The pursuit is referred to only in general terms in the Spanish: those familiar with the sport and the poetic tradition would understand that the quarry was the heron (as it is, explicitly, in many of the falconry poems): I had specified both birds in the translation. Hawking for the heron was regarded as perhaps the noblest and most thrilling form of the sport: the heron, with its large wings and light body, could rise in sheer, almost perpendicular rings, and when alarmed would make for the upper air; the falcon, in wide, sweeping circles because of its greater weight, strength, and speed, would gradually overtake the heron, perhaps in the very clouds, soaring high above to dive for the quarry.

The first version of this translation, published in *Poetry* in August, 1958, was done in another manner, as follows:

OF FALCONRY

a lo divino

A falcon, no feather adroop,
oversailing the heron of love
in thrilling crescendo above:
—a prize!—on the plumage I swoop!

To pounce on the bird quick and true
in flurries of high interplay,
I soared by so dizzy a way
I was barely a guess in the blue.
Even so, at the zenith of hope
I hung numb, until buoyant on love
in thrilling crescendo above
—a prize!—on the plumage I swoop!

At the dizziest pitch of my flight,
my eyes!—they were dazzled and blind.
So my magnificent find
was made amid thickness of night.
Without knowing how, I swung up
(for at stake was a trophy of love)
in thrilling crescendo above
till—a prize!—on the plumage I swoop!

As higher and higher I rose
in sudden and surging ascent,
the more I was conscious *I can't*,
the weaker and weaker I was
and despaired of the quarry: no hope
for any pursuer!—and dove
in thrilling crescendo above
till—a prize!—on the plumage I swoop!

Who knows how it ends or begins?
One flight? or a thousand I fly?
Who longs for delight in the sky
whatever he challenges, wins.
Here's no misadventure of hope
(high hope for the heron of love):
in thrilling crescendo above
—a prize!—on the plumage I swoop!

Madrigal (pp. 40–41)

This poignant and melancholy poem, which Brenan finds "the tenderest of his *canciones*" cannot be dated precisely but would seem to be early, conceivably belonging even to a period before the imprisonment. Without the rhythmic velocity of the greater poems, this has the feeling of a pastoral piece by Garcilaso *a lo divino*—it is more than likely, in fact, that the device of shepherd-and-tree was suggested by its use in Sebastián de Córdoba's versions. Alonso points out that in some ways this poem resembles the anonymous fifteenth-century English *Quia Amore Langueo*. The source has only recently been found by José Blecua in the Bibliothèque Nationale. At first glance it would seem that St. John had followed his source quite closely; actually his remodeling of the material has been subtle and expressive, as we can see by comparing his version, so much richer in pathos, drama, and significance, with the popular love song he adapted, and which might be translated, to show how many lines are identical, as follows:

THE YOUNG SHEPHERD

Once a young shepherd went off to despond:
how could he dance again? how could he sing?
Firmly his thoughts to his shepherdess cling,
with love in his heart like a ruinous wound.

Not sighing "Forgotten!" he went to despond;
"Forgotten?"—no chance of it, no. What distressed
was thinking it too much a suitor's, his breast,
with love in his heart like a ruinous wound.

The shepherd lad murmured, "The curse that I've found!
For how can I bear it, the day of farewell?
My life's in her presence; there only can dwell
with love in my heart like a ruinous wound."

He imagines himself as a wanderer, bound
from his beautiful shepherdess—driven afar;
and lies stretched on the ground there and never will stir,
with love in his heart like a ruinous wound.

Song of the Soul (pp. 42–45)

These *coplas* were said to have been composed in prison. Alonso finds the poem strange in every way: he thinks the form *fonte* (instead of the normal *fuente*) of the first line indicates an ancient dialectal assonance with the *noche* of the short line—from this he concludes that the original form of the *villancico* had three short lines instead of a long line and a short line. Probably, he suggests, St. John was developing an old *villancico* from the west, now lost—but developing it, most strangely of all, not in the rhythms of folk poetry but in that fashionable and highbrow importation, the Italian hendecasyllable. For further peculiarities, cf. PSJ, p. 118 and *passim*. Brenan finds this "disturbing" poem "one of the most original and beautiful"; he sees in it a highly independent handling of the *villancico*: St. John "has taken, as the custom was, his *estribillo* from an old popular song, altering it perhaps a little; then he has shortened the stanzas to two lines each and let the weight of the poem rest on the peculiarly insinuating refrain, which acts on the reader with the effect of a whispered incantation." The symbolism of flowing water, PSJ reminds us, was common in the mystics: certain Franciscan writers used for the Trinity the triple symbol of fountain, river, and sea.

Ballads (pp. 46–81)

The group of nine ballads, and the ballad that follows on the psalm *Super flumina Babylonis,* were composed in prison. Some at least were dictated by St. John from memory, immediately after his escape, to one of the nuns who gave him shelter—they were described then as "so sublime and devout that they seemed to enkindle the reader." But these poems on theological themes, in the rhythms and language of the popular ballads (the same rime in *fa* is carried relentlessly through all nine) have not often come in for such praise: they are likely to be thought of as among the poet's more perfunctory pieces.

Yet Dámaso Alonso, himself a poet of distinction, speaks up for them: he declares that in their very rusticity and sameness they have a certain transparency, a tangy freshness or harsh charm.

Without and With Mainstay (pp. 84–87)

Neither this poem nor the one that follows is found in the Sanlúcar codex or the first published edition of the poems. Though included in the Codex of Jaén, their attribution to St. John of the Cross is not beyond question. For this poem, no definite model has been found; it seems probable enough that both theme and development were inventions of the author.

The Lucky Days (pp. 88–93)

Cf. comment on the preceding poem. *The Lucky Days* is based on a poem published in 1580 with an almost identical initial theme: a poem that refers, with a certain ambiguity, to idealized human love. The author, Pedro de Padilla, five years later himself became a Carmelite. St. John (if he is the author) develops de Padilla's theme *a lo divino*.

Divine Word (pp. 94–95)

Alonso finds no irrefragable evidence for the authenticity of either of the little verses on these pages. St. John is reported to have urged the religious under his direction to compose, during times of recreation, verses that would enkindle divine love. *Divine Word* is said to have been improvised by the saint for a Christmas celebration in the monastery of Granada when he was prior there.

The Capsule of Perfection (pp. 94–95)

Attributed to St. John by P. Estéban de San José in 1667.

The Spiritual Canticle (Revised Version) (pp. 98–115)

Cf. the Notes to "The Spiritual Canticle" (pp. 2–17). In the revised version, which appears in the Codex of Jaén, the eleventh stanza

"Appear here at my side . . .") is added; otherwise both versions are the same up to the beginning of the sixteenth stanza ("Now that the bloom uncloses . . ."). The last seven stanzas are in the same order in both versions. Stanzas in between are altered in the interests of a more logical and systematic account of the progress from the state of Spiritual Betrothal to the loftier state of Spiritual Marriage. In the first version, fifteen stanzas are concerned with the Betrothal of the soul to God (from the first appearance of the Bridegroom in the twelfth stanza to the twenty-seventh stanza, which begins "She enters, the bride!"). In the second version, only five stanzas, beginning at the same point as in the first version, are given to this stage. The other ten, from the fifteenth ("Our bed, a couch of roses . . .") to the twenty-fourth ("But thought me, cheek and brow . . .") have been transferred to the state of Spiritual Marriage, since they refer to a security of bliss apparently thought beyond the capacities of the earlier state. Four stanzas of the first version would describe misgivings of the soul in the state of Spiritual Marriage ("Girls of Jerusalem . . . islands in her chase . . ." "Wings flickering here and there . . . Off you go!" are transferred to the lower state, more likely to be troubled by such apprehensions. This is all to the good, since as P. Silverio has said it leaves the two states "much more precisely differentiated and clearly described." But these schematic gains have perhaps been achieved at too great a cost. These Notes are not the place for a thorough study of the two versions—but readers will surely notice that though in theory the continuity of the revision is better, in the fact of the poem it sometimes falters. In the revised version, for example, the little foxes and the chilling wind are brought in too abruptly after the ecstasy of the preceding stanzas, and the entrance of the bride into the garden (the twenty-second stanza) is not only less dramatic (since in mid-speech) but even anticlimactic, since she has been described as sleeping securely in the stanza before. The apparent inconsistencies of the first version can even be defended : the too great happiness of the Betrothed (the mention of the flowery bed, for example) can be seen as anticipations, visions, longings—the garden, when she does finally enter it, is described as *deseado* ("longed for"). The apprehensive stanzas in the first account of the Spiritual Marriage can be explained on the grounds that in the poem itself they sound by no means so ominous as the explications would have them ; and in any event the Spiritual Marriage is attainable in this life, and hence is not a condition of unshakable security.